LOW STRESS INVESTING

10 Simple Steps to a Worry-Free Portfolio

C. Andrew Millard

Trade Street Publishing ■ Tryon, North Carolina

Low-Stress Investing: 10 Simple Steps to a Worry-Free
Portfolio © 2002 by C. Andrew Millard

Trade Street Publishing
Post Office Box 774
Tryon, North Carolina 28782 USA

Main Street Financial Group, Inc. has applied to the
U.S. government's Patent and Trademark Office (PTO)
for the trademark to the phrase "Low-Stress Investing."
All rights reserved pending trademark approval.

Cover photo by Chuck Abernathy
Book design by Sara Patton
Printed in the USA
All unattributed quotes are by the author.

Publisher's Cataloging-in-Publication
(Provided by Quality Books, Inc.)

Millard, C. Andrew, 1957–
    Low-stress investing : 10 simple steps to a worry-free
portfolio / C. Andrew Millard. — 1st ed.
        p. cm.
    Includes bibliographical references and index.
    ISBN 0-9720983-0-5

    1. Investments.   2. Finance, Personal.   I. Title.

HG 4521.M55 2002   332.6
                                    QBI02-200442

WARNING – DISCLAIMER

This book is designed to provide accurate and authoritative information regarding the subject matter covered. It is not intended as specific investment advice to any individual. If professional advice or other expert assistance is required, you should consult with a competent professional (see Chapter 4, "Are You a Gardener or a Produce Buyer?").

This book contains performance data, and the presentation of such data is not meant to imply that similar results will be achieved in the future. Past performance is no indication of future results. The data is provided for illustrative and comparative purposes. Performance data using a wide variety of time periods is provided, and rather than focusing on the specific time periods or return figures, the reader should focus on the underlying principles instead.

Every effort has been made to make this guide as complete and accurate as possible. However, *there may be mistakes*, both typographical and in content. Therefore, this text should be used only as a general guide and not as the ultimate source of investment information. All facts and figures provided are from sources that the author believes reliable and are assumed to be correct, but cannot be guaranteed as to accuracy. Furthermore, this book contains information that is current only up to the printing date.

The purpose of this guide is to educate and entertain. The author and publisher shall have neither liability nor responsibility to any person or entity with respect to any loss or damage caused, or alleged to have been caused, directly or indirectly from this book.

If you do not wish to be bound by the above, you may return this book to the publisher for a full refund.

CONTENTS

Chapter 7
THE BEAUTY OF MUTUAL FUNDS

Part Three
STEP BY STEP

Chapter 8
PLANNING YOUR PORTFOLIO

Chapter 9
BUILDING AND MAINTAINING YOUR PORTFOLIO

Dedicated to my parents, Bob and Joan Millard. They taught me that I could accomplish anything I set my mind to — and then dared me to go out and do it. The legacy they have given my siblings and me is the purest, truest form of wealth.

ACKNOWLEDGMENTS

I have a number of people to thank for helping make this book a reality. First and foremost are my wife Sharon and our thirteen-year-old son Drew, whose ideas and perspective never cease to amaze us.

My friend Carroll Brady has been of immeasurable help in every aspect of the project, especially editing the manuscript from a reader's point of view; Rev. Dr. Ronald Stegall and Liz Malloy have also contributed in this regard. Scott Muchmore and his staff at Mountain Inn and Suites in Hendersonville, NC provided me a quiet place to write when I needed it.

Several professional contacts have assisted as well. Nick Worontzoff of Fidelity's Institutional Brokerage Group has supported me in countless ways for years. Also from Fidelity, Michael Patti and Greg Lotardo have proofed specific chapters for accuracy, as has Scott Spalding of PIMCO.

Any work like this one relies heavily on source material, and *Low-Stress Investing* is no exception. I wish to thank Roger Gibson, Bill Bachrach and David Bach for permission to quote some of their work. Thomson Financial, makers of the *InvestmentView* software program, have always provided reliable, accurate and unbiased information on mutual funds and indexes, and I appreciate their allowing me to use information obtained from them throughout the book.

Dr. Donald Moine deserves special recognition. His widely respected column in MorningstarAdvisor.com prompted me to write this book. He has contributed encouragement, professional insight and invaluable suggestions. I greatly appreciate his support.

The professional appearance of this book is the result of a creative team of individuals: Graham Van Dixhorn of Susan Kendrick Writing, Kathi Dunn of Dunn+Associates, and Sara Patton of Sara Patton Design Services. Each has been a delight to work with. My old friend Robert Frost and his colleague Fran DaCanal also deserve a special thank-you.

I am also grateful to Stephen Brady, Rhett Giddings, and Tripp Flack, my business partners and friends, for their support in this endeavor. Our staff at Main Street Financial Group deserve my deep gratitude as well. I especially want to recognize my former assistants, Melinda Champion and Crystal Yoder, for their loyalty and devotion. Their belief in me is a constant source of strength.

Finally, I wish to thank my clients for entrusting me with their life savings; for listening to my advice; for supporting me as I have come to learn the truths expressed in this book; for enriching my life with their friendships; and for enabling me to make a living while maintaining the balance that is so important to all of us.

It truly is a wonderful life.

LOW STRESS INVESTING

10 Simple Steps to a Worry-Free Portfolio

You can't buy happiness,
but you can rent
financial security.

Keeping Money in Perspective

DOES INVESTING STRESS YOU OUT?

- Do you worry about your investments?

- Has the unpredictability of the stock market paralyzed you with indecision?

- Are you angered and confused by corporate scandals?

- Do you wonder if your portfolio is *really right* for you?

- Are you reliant on brokers or analysts whose motives you question?

- Do you find it hard to devote *enough* time to maintaining your investment portfolio? Do you spend *too much* time on it?

- Do you hope for financial security but wonder if you're really on track to achieve it?

If you answered yes to any of these questions, you're in the right place. Low-Stress Investing can remove all those worries from your mind and restore balance to your life.

We'll get to the details a little later, but let's start by placing money in its proper perspective.

BALANCE IN ALL THINGS

How important is money in the big scheme of things?

If you're like most people, money is probably less important to you than your family, friends, liberty, quality of life, and your spiritual and physical well being. Being rich, owning the biggest house or the fanciest car—these notions probably hold little appeal for you.

If you had your choice, how would you spend most of your time? Let your imagination run wild. Some possible answers: Stay at home with your loved ones. Lie on the beach. Hike the Appalachian Trail. RV across our great country. Volunteer for religious or community causes. Climb Mount Everest. Play golf. Write a book. Your answer will be unique to you, but you get the picture.

What do you worry about? Your kids or other members of your family? Problems at home or work? Unrest in the world?

Money?

Sure you do. Studies have repeatedly shown money to be our biggest source of worry. Everybody worries about money, from the homeless beggar to the wealthiest tycoon. The real problem occurs when money becomes an object in itself. What an irony that so many rich people are miserable while so many of limited means are carefree and happy.

The inescapable conclusion is that many affluent individuals are unhappy *because of their money.*

This is just the opposite of how it should be. Money should enhance your quality of life, not detract from it. It should allow you to buy necessities and luxuries, a nice home, quality health care, and freedom to live as you please. There should be a sense of inner peace from knowing that you don't have to constantly work just to put food on the table, that you can afford to send your kids to college, that you won't be a burden to your children in later years.

When I see affluent people who are unhappy or confused, it often seems they feel the need to live and invest like a "rich" person: spending freely and investing aggressively. In good times, they're riding high, but in bad times, they worry about keeping it together. Even when things are going great, they worry about possible disaster right around the corner.

> **What an irony that so many rich people are miserable while so many of limited means are carefree and happy.**

In short, they have their priorities mixed up.

Which brings us to the whole point of this book: we want to have the peace of mind that comes with being financially secure. So why do so many of us manage our investments in a way that *increases our stress level?*

TOO MUCH ADVICE

Everybody wants to tell you how to invest. Pundits and prophets are everywhere: on TV, in the papers, in magazines, at dinner parties. I frequently have clients, friends and even strangers tell me where *they* think the market is headed in the next few months. (Frankly, I myself have no idea.) And why shouldn't they? Everybody else has an opinion—why can't they?

The problem is that when you allow yourself to get sucked into the modern investment culture, it's very hard to find any peace of mind. Why? *Information overload!*

It's impossible to keep up with every analyst's recommendations—and even if you could, you'd tear your hair out trying to decide which ones to believe. Worse is the inescapable fact

> **It's impossible to keep up with every analyst's recommendations—and even if you could, you'd tear your hair out trying to decide which ones to believe.**

that all those talking heads are making money from your confusion. Your uncertainty creates a need for them—even as they themselves compound that uncertainty.

Then there are those investors who have taken advantage of the explosion of Internet resources by managing their own investments through an online brokerage house such as Ameritrade, Datek, Schwab, or any of the myriad other options. They spend hours and hours sorting through a constant din of information. And yet, they are still at the mercy of the prophets and pundits, because prophets and pundits *are the ones making all the noise.*

Worse still, everyone seems to be singing a different tune at the same time. It's all very loud, very confusing—and quite meaningless.

MY STORY

Balance is important to me.

Although I'm in the money business, money isn't my life— my family is. I come from a family of educators; when the time came for me to enter the working world following college and graduate school, I was drawn to the classroom. After seven years teaching junior high school, I took the next step and studied to be an administrator. I soon became assistant principal at the largest high school in a 54-school system.

But my wife and I wanted to raise our son in a small town. So after a brief search, I found myself—at age 35—in my dream job: principal of a brand-new consolidated high school in a beautiful western North Carolina community. We had found our home.

Things don't always work out the way we expect them to, and such was the case with my "dream job." The pressures of consolidating two rival schools combined with long hours to reverse my priorities—family became second to career. After a year I was transferred to a smaller school; after two years I was ready for a new job.

By now we were settled into our new community. I had no intention of uprooting my family just so I could start the same process all over again. What to do? Possessing a good attitude and little else, I looked for opportunities within my chosen community.

Our area is a haven for active retirees in need of financial planning and investment help. While we were overloaded with stockbrokers, it appeared there were almost no true financial *advisors*. Thus began my new career as an independent investment consultant.

That was eight years ago. I was a school principal who knew nothing about investing—I had no education or training in the financial world, just a desire to help people secure their financial future. I turned down an offer from a major national brokerage firm because I wanted to be free to serve clients in the way I saw fit. So I took courses, studied, obtained the necessary licenses and went to work.

Blissfully ignorant of the behavior expected of a stockbroker, I set about researching what constitutes successful investing— *not* how to sell investment products. The fact that I had no clients was a blessing in disguise, because I was able to devote almost full time to my search. I reasoned that if I learned to do things the right way, clients would follow.

And what do you suppose I found? Information overload! I started by studying the financial media: newspapers, magazines, TV and radio programs, and the Internet. What a jumbled mess that was! All the pundits seemed to make sense, but they were all saying different things. There was no way to tell who was right and who was wrong.

Many of the "training programs" available for investment professionals were just as useless. They mostly focused on the best ways to sell products and overcome the objections of potential buyers. There was a lot of emphasis on which products paid the highest commissions to the broker—and very little emphasis on what was best for the investor. When they finally did get around to looking at portfolio management, the focus was almost exclusively on the stock market, with a few bonds thrown in.

The competing information screaming from all corners of the investment world drowned out the still, small voice of sound investment practice. But I kept digging. After several years of examining and rejecting the numerous systems, gurus, methods and theories, I gradually came to learn—and understand— the truth.

And the clients did follow. I now have a thriving advisory practice. I help clients manage millions of dollars by applying the principals in this book. Neither they nor I worry about their investments. We check them periodically and make adjustments as needed. Because the portfolios don't require a great deal of time, we can work on other areas of their financial lives as well.

> **Low-Stress Investing is based on decades of proven, common-sense history that anyone can verify.**

My clients are retirees, baby boomers, middle-aged people, and young families. They work, volunteer, travel, hike, play golf, and spend time with loved ones. Their lives—and mine—are in balance. It's a wonderful feeling.

Now you can have that feeling, too. I wrote this book to save you the trouble and stress of learning what I have learned.

The answer to my question—what constitutes successful investing?—was always out there. In fact it was clear as a bell. The information discussed in this book is neither new nor revolutionary—it has been freely available for years. But it's hidden like a needle in a haystack, completely obscured under piles of competing, confusing, and often useless information.

To make matters even more confusing, much of the investment establishment has a vested interest in your *not* knowing the principles behind Low-Stress Investing—because you may realize you don't need their help as much as they'd like you to. And although many investment professionals are aware of this information, many refuse to *accept* it—because it calls into question the advice they have been giving for years.

WOULDN'T IT BE GREAT NOT TO WORRY ABOUT YOUR INVESTMENTS?

Low-Stress Investing delivers just what the name implies: an approach to investing that lets you sleep peacefully at night. Low-Stress Investing gives you several distinct advantages:

- It's simple.
- It's tailored to your precise situation and needs.
- It's based on decades of market research.
- It spreads your risk as well as your opportunities.
- It's easy to establish and maintain.

- It doesn't require constant attention.
- It provides an automatic process for buying low and selling high.
- It allows you to ignore the prophets and pundits.
- It's cheap (little or no trading commissions). And . . .
- It works!

What all this means is that you can set up your investment plan and then go live your life. Spend your time as you please. Concentrate your mind and efforts on the fulfilling aspects of life. Your Low-Stress portfolio requires only a few minutes of your attention several times a year.

WHAT IT'S NOT

Here's what Low-Stress Investing is *not*:

- It's not a get-rich-quick scheme.
- It's not a method for timing the markets.
- It's not a system for picking sure-fire stock winners.
- It's not reliant on a market guru to tell you what to do .
- It's not a "secrets-of-the-pros" investing system. Low-Stress Investing is based on decades of proven, common-sense history that anyone can verify.

WHAT YOU'LL HAVE TO GIVE UP

Nothing's perfect, and so it is with Low-Stress Investing. There are some things you will have to forego if you are to reap its many benefits. Here's what you'll have to give up:

- The elusive goal of "beating the market."
- Expectations of annual returns in the triple digits— maybe even double digits.
- Watching the ticker tape on television.

- The temptation to time the markets.

- The tendency to buy the latest stock touted in the financial media.

- The comfort of following the crowd.

- Belief in market prophets and pundits.

- Bragging rights at cocktail parties (at least in very bullish years). Don't worry, though — empty boasting may well be replaced by a quiet sense of self-satisfaction.

WHAT YOU STAND TO GAIN

I can't promise that your portfolio will outperform the market—or even your brother-in-law's IRA. But if you follow the Low-Stress Investing method, you should enjoy some very meaningful benefits:

- A clear-eyed view of what you can reasonably expect from your portfolio.

- An all-weather portfolio that should withstand market storms.

- More time to spend on the important things.

- Greater peace of mind.

- A sense of control.

- A more secure financial future.

Curious? Read on . . .

PART ONE

The Problem:
Stacking Boards

Despite the lessons of history and logic, most people subconsciously assume that recent market trends will continue permanently into the future. That assumption is a huge obstacle to investing sucess. Open your mind. Prepare to look at investing in a new and different way.

Myths of Traditional Investing

Conventional investment wisdom is driven by several common myths. Because they go unchallenged by the popular press, investors are slaves to them. There are at least four of them . . .

MYTH #1: "EVERYBODY'S GETTING RICH EXCEPT ME"

It's not true! Don't let them fool you!

Ever see this TV commercial? A suave-looking guy is sitting in a warmly lit den reading a leading daily financial paper *in slow motion.* (Why slow motion?) He doesn't speak, but a progression of printed tag lines fades in and out at the bottom of the screen; the message goes something like this:

Subscribed in March . . .
Sold short in August . . .
Bought in November . . .

And then, as the man slowly looks up from his paper with a sly grin on his face, we read the final tag line:

Wonders . . . why he didn't do this sooner?

Here's another one (this one I've seen so many times I have it memorized): A portly gentleman is reading another well-known investment paper as he reclines on a pool float in some stylized body of water. As the water level rises and falls at the appropriate times, the announcer intones:

> *The market goes up: you make money . . .*
> *The market goes down: you make money . . .*
> *It's nice to be a Barron's subscriber.*

Oh, brother! The clear implication is that getting rich in the market is easy if only you're smart enough to subscribe to the right publication and read it religiously. All you need to know is what to buy and sell, and when to buy and sell it. Seems like so many others are doing it—why can't you?

Put your mind at ease. It simply is not true that everybody except you has gotten rich in the stock market. The false culture created around advertising and the financial press just makes it *look* that way. But it's not reality.

True, during the technology boom of the mid- to late nineties, many stocks spiraled wildly higher in a seemingly endless frenzy of spectacular returns. And many lucky individuals got very wealthy. There were just two problems:

First, much of the new wealth wasn't based on anything real. It was based on the unrealistic hope that many high tech companies would reap incredible profits *someday*. Eventually, the upward frenzy became a monster that fed on itself. Many companies had no realistic profits—or even prospects—to justify their inflated prices. It was bound to end badly.

The second problem is the real kicker. Unless investors were smart enough—or lucky enough—to sell at the right time, they lost much (or all) of that phantom wealth when the market came to its senses. But most *didn't* sell—because they were blinded by the frenzy. So while investors may have gotten rich for a while on paper, most aren't so rich now.

Sad to say, the cardinal rule of investing—*buy low, sell high*—is regularly broken by the vast majority of investors. If you use the Low-Stress Investing method, you may never break this rule again.

> **The cardinal rule of investing—buy low, sell high—is regularly broken by the vast majority of investors.**

MYTH #2: THE MARKET GURU

This myth has been promulgated by brokerage houses and the financial media for decades. It tells us that there are a few exceptional individuals who are able to read the future. A guru can supposedly tell when the stock market will tumble and, once it has tumbled, when it will recover. The problem is, just like in the old story, the emperor has no clothes.

One market analyst successfully predicted the 1987 October stock market crash one week in advance. This person attained instant guru status, which she has largely enjoyed ever since. Unfortunately for those who have followed her advice, she has been wrong at least as often as she has been right.

But she always makes her predictions with conviction and urgency, and she backs them up with statistical evidence. Still, she's frequently wrong.

Why do investors pay attention to such nonsense? For one thing, because the media monster must be fed. Think about the countless hours that must be filled to keep the 24-hour financial news networks on the air. Then consider the hundreds of pages that comprise the financial newspapers on an average day, not to mention the millions of words that fill the investment magazines and investing web sites.

What's more, major brokerage houses, money managers—and the gurus themselves—have a vested interest in keeping investors dependent upon them for advice. They make millions in salaries, fees, and newsletter subscriptions by sharing their insights with us.

And how have they done? Their records should be great, right? Wrong. Peter Lynch, one of the greatest stock market investors of all time, gave his opinion on the subject to PBS's *Frontline* in 1996: "I don't remember anybody predicting the market right more than once, and they predict a lot."[1]

MYTH #3: TIMING THE MARKET

"Yes, Frank, I think the recession is over, and you're going to see stronger earnings by many of the bellwether companies. With interest rates at blah blah blah blah blah blah . . ."

This inane conversation takes place in some form or other several times a day on television's financial shows. Apparently, no one stops to point out that market timing doesn't work consistently—never has, never will.

The key word in that last paragraph is "consistently." Sure, timing works on occasion—even a blind squirrel finds an acorn every now and again, as they say. The trick is to make it work *year after year*—and that's also where the trouble lies.

In his excellent book, *Asset Allocation: Balancing Financial Risk*, Roger Gibson puts forth a much more complete and convincing discussion on this subject than we can here. One quote especially bears repeating:

> *The realities of the marketplace . . . stubbornly persist. Research studies repeatedly show that most money managers underperform the market on average over time, and those*

---

[1] You can view a transcript of the entire interview online at: http://www.pbs.org/wgbh/pages/frontline/shows/betting/pros/lynch.html

who do outperform the market in one time period do not have a better than even chance of outperforming the market in the next time period. This is not a surprising conclusion. Professionals populate the marketplace, and by definition, the majority cannot outperform the average. Given the transaction costs and management fees incurred in attempting to do so, it is expected that in the future most money managers will continue to underperform the market as a whole.[2]

What makes the stock market move up or down? History has given us the answer over and over: *unforeseen events.* There is no other possible answer. Think about it. What other answer could there be? *Foreseen* events? If so, then those amazing market gurus would foresee the future and *consistently* make the right moves. Name one who has.

How much sense does it make to think that you—or anyone—can accurately predict something that *by its very nature* is unpredictable?

One reason so many investors find it easy to believe in market timing is their apparent short-term success at it. Take the mid- to late 1990s for example. Many new investors got involved in stocks during this period. Lo and behold, their bet paid off handsomely. They made money—in many cases, a lot of money.

Some investors were under the false impression that their natural gift for market timing was responsible for the windfall. But in fact, it was almost impossible *not* to make great profits in stocks during that period—the vast majority of stocks just kept going up, up, up.

---

[2] Gibson, Roger C. *Asset Allocation: Balancing Financial Risk,* New York: McGraw-Hill, 2000.

Our human nature causes us to take credit for decisions that work out; conversely, we tend to blame something or someone else when our decisions turn out badly. As a result, many investors — amateurs and professionals alike — have fooled themselves into thinking that their good decisions are the result of talent and brains . . . and their poor decisions are the result of bad luck or bad advice.

Finally, investors have a natural *desire* to believe that they can time the market successfully. It's so easy to see market patterns in hindsight, it's only natural to think we should be able to see them in advance—or while they are occurring.

> **Your life as an investor will be much less stressful if you stop trying to accomplish the impossible.**

New clients sometimes tell me, "When you see the fund *start* to go down, sell it." They assume I can read market patterns in real time, and that once a security starts to depreciate, it will continue to do so until I read a change in the pattern—and neatly buy back in. It's always painful to see the look on their faces when I tell them the truth.

Believe me: your life as an investor will be much less stressful if you *stop trying to accomplish the impossible.*

MYTH #4: THE STOCK-PICKER

Okay, so market timing doesn't work. But is it possible, by skillfully buying the stocks of excellent companies, to out-perform the market for a while? Almost certainly. How likely is it that a stock-picker can continue outperforming the market for an extended period? Not very.

Let's say that you, as a stock investor, wanted to beat the return of the stock market as a whole. If you could have anything you wished for to maximize your chances of success, what would you want?

You would probably want to have knowledge of how the markets worked; you'd want to have direct access to the CEOs of your target companies; you'd probably even want to visit those companies and see their operations up close. While you're wishing, you might as well wish for a staff of professionals with degrees in economics and finance who would support your efforts. Finally, you'd want the best, latest technology for crunching the numbers and making your trades. A smart investor with all these tools at her command would have an excellent chance of beating the market, right?

There *are* smart investors with all those tools—and more —at their command. They are called mutual fund managers.

Mutual funds are run by some of the smartest investors in America. If anybody can consistently outperform the market averages, they should. But the historical record is not very encouraging for those of us with fewer tools than the average fund manager.

During the five-year period ending on December 31, 2001, there were a total of 2,676 mutual funds that dealt primarily with U.S. stocks.[3] (For the purposes of this little study, we will not include any S&P 500 index funds.) Each of those funds had a manager, a man or woman whose job was to:

- Scour the universe of available stocks,

---

[3] Source for all mutual fund figures: Thomson Financial's *Investment-View*™ software, version 9.0, 12/31/01 update. Includes the following fund categories: Aggressive Growth; Equity Income; Growth & Income; Growth – Domestic; Mid Cap; Small Cap; and all stock sector categories.

- Find the ones that have the best chances of appreciating more rapidly or dramatically than the others,
- Buy them, and
- Later sell them at the point of maximum profit.

If you had to guess, how many of those managers would you say outperformed the S&P 500 in 1997, the first year of this five-year period? If even *half* of them outperformed—a reasonable expectation based on luck alone—that would be 1,338 outperformers.

Try 299. That's right, barely 11% of stock mutual funds had a better overall return than the S&P in 1997. Considering all the advantages those fund managers enjoy, that's a pretty poor record.

But what about the 299 that did beat the average? Was their outperformance the result of skill—or luck? Perhaps a good way to answer that question would be to look at the following year, 1998. Remember, a great stock picker should deliver superior returns *consistently.*

Of the 299 funds that outperformed in 1997, a mere 79 were able to follow up with outperformance in 1998. That's less than 3% of the total we started with. Three percent!

The numbers continue to deteriorate each year until, by the end of 2001, only *six funds* had outperformed for five years in a row—less than one quarter of one percent of the overall group.

Care to bet that you can outperform the market, or pick a fund that can? Sounds pretty stressful to me.

Does all this mean that mutual fund managers are failures? Not at all. In fact, mutual funds are my preferred investment vehicle. Sound inconsistent? *Only if your goal is to beat the market.* And, as we have just seen, beating the market is a myth.

If your goal is to earn good, solid returns with a minimum of stress and anxiety, mutual funds make perfect sense. We'll discuss them more completely in Chapter Seven, "The Beauty of Mutual Funds."

There are plenty of other myths having to do with money and financial planning. David Bach, author of *Smart Women Finish Rich* and *Smart Couples Finish Rich*, discusses a number of them in his books and seminars. If you want to enrich your life in more ways than one, Bach is an excellent resource. You can find him online at www.finishrich.com.

FOLLOWING THE CROWD OFF THE CLIFF

If your friends told you to jump off a cliff, would you do it?

As kids, we learned not to blindly follow the crowd. But that's exactly what most investors do. There are several reasons:

- Psychology—the lure of beating the market is strong.

- Sociology—we hate the idea of being average or (even worse) below average.

- The media—imagine how hard it would be to attract viewers, readers and advertisers if the futility of beating the market were actively publicized. So the media *actively promotes* all four myths.

- Temptation—past trends are so obvious in hindsight, looking forward shouldn't be hard.

And perhaps the most irresistible reason:

- Everybody else seems to be doing it.

In a very real sense, we're like a herd of cattle stampeding off a cliff. The crowd does it wrong, so we do it wrong.

Remember Myth #1: Everybody's getting rich except you? The reality is that everybody's walking over the cliff — including you.

Mutual fund managers really are some of the smartest investors in America. If they can't beat the market, what makes us think we can?

If you're still convinced that you can beat the market — and that it's important for you to try — then there's nothing I can do for you. You might as well throw this book in the trash right now and get on with it. Good-bye, and good luck.

Still here? Good!

Read this — understand it — believe it:

> **You don't have to beat the market to be a successful investor. There's no need to try.**

Facing this truth will do wonders for your stress level. Now, let's go to the next step . . .

Stuck on Stocks

Americans love the stock market.

In fact, for most investors, investing *equals* stocks. Probably 95% of the investing questions people ask me involve stocks or the stock market:

- " What's the market doing today?"
- " When do you think Cisco is coming back?"
- " Have you heard about ABC Communications?"
- " Is now a good time to buy stocks?"
- " Hey, how 'bout that scandal at XYZ Corp.?"

There's nothing wrong with the questions — they just point up our obvious fixation on stocks. Let's look at some more evidence:

- Out of a universe of 11,902 mutual funds, 63% are primarily focused on stocks—that's 7,474 funds.

- As of January 26, 2002, Zacks.com offered for sale a full 449 research reports on Microsoft stock, written by various analysts. A recent search for "stock analysts" on Google.com turned up about 990,000 responses.

- According to Idiotsguide.com, there are over 140 discount brokers to choose from—that's not to mention the scores of full service brokerage firms.

■ Over seven million Americans trade stocks over the Internet.

This fixation on stocks is a huge obstacle to investing success for many people. They think of stocks as the only road to investing success—and they believe the only measure of success is to beat the averages. We have already seen that beating the averages is an elusive phantom, so . . .

WHY ARE WE STUCK ON STOCKS?

■ The deep-seated love of capitalism.

■ The desire to be a part of a success story.

■ The promise of great wealth.

■ The influence of the media—they push stocks, so we love stocks. (Or is it the other way around—we love, so they push?)

■ Force of habit—it's what we're used to.

■ The long-term stock averages.

All these reasons are valid. But *staying* stuck on stocks— and stocks alone—can cause some real problems.

THE PROBLEM WITH HISTORICAL AVERAGES

Stocks have been a great way to invest for a very long time. But the numbers can be very, very misleading:

■ $10,000 invested in the S&P 500 at the end of 1971 (with dividends and capital gains reinvested) would have been worth $396,409 on January 1, 2000—an annual average return of 14.05%.[4]

---

[4] Unless otherwise noted, all market figures in this book are derived from Thomson Financial's *InvestmentView*™ software, version 9.0.

That's good, but this is even better:

- $10,000 invested in the NASDAQ Composite at its inception in 1971 would have been worth $517,455 on January 1, 2000—for an eye-popping average return of 15.14%.

- If you had held that $517,455 NASDAQ portfolio for an additional two and a half years, until June 30, 2002, you would have . . . $186,061.

That's right. In 30 short months, you would have lost over half of your investment. But your *average* annual return still would have been 10.06%. Does that make you feel any better about the loss? Didn't think so.

- And, oh yes, your S&P nest egg would have been worth $275,713. Better than the NASDAQ, but still off 30% from its high two and a half years earlier.

And if, like many stock investors, your investments performed *worse* than the averages . . . ouch!

That's the problem with relying on "average annual return" numbers. They look fine on paper—and in theory—but they're cold comfort after a couple of bad years. The unsettling reality is that *there's no way to predict when the bad years will come.*

PROJECTING THE PAST INTO THE FUTURE

There's another problem with using historical returns, and you've seen it a thousand times. It's written in small print in every mutual fund ad and prospectus: *Past performance is no guarantee of future results.* The regulations require funds to send you this message—because the message is absolutely true.

And what do most investors do? *Rear-view mirror investing.* We buy the fund that was last year's best performer, or has the

What do most investors do? Rear-view mirror investing.

best trailing three-year or five-year record. Or we buy the stock that has tripled in the last year—if so many investors like it, surely it must continue to appreciate dramatically.

But the past performance of a stock or fund really is a poor indicator of its future growth. Next time you read that disclaimer, let it sink in. Believe it—it's true.

MARKET TIMING IN THE REAL WORLD

How many people do you know who invested all their money in the NASDAQ in 1971, and sold on January 1, 2000? That's right—none. Because that's not how real people invest. For one thing, real people can't invest in averages. And real people seldom invest at the very beginning of anything. They're afraid to buy, so they watch the market go up, up, up. When they're finally convinced it will go up forever, they jump in.

When the market starts to fall, they hold on. Why shouldn't they? It's probably just a momentary dip. But if the market keeps sinking, they start to worry. Finally, they become fearful of losing everything, so they sell. Or maybe they hold on—and kick themselves for not having sold at the top.

Real people frequently buy *high* and sell *low*. It's not their fault—it's just human nature. But talk about stressful! Low-Stress Investing will give you a method for avoiding this trap.

THE TRUTH ABOUT THE DOW

There seems to be a common misconception that the long-term annual average for stocks has been around 12%, forever. Not true.

Ready for a shock? Since the inception of the Dow Jones Industrial Average in 1928 through the end of 2001, the Dow averaged an annual return of just 5.16%. That's right, 5.16% per year, from the beginning.[5]

(Note: This figure doesn't include reinvested dividends, because Dow Jones didn't start tracking them with the index until around 1960. One could reasonably add another 3–3.5% per year onto the 5.16% figure for reinvested dividends. That would bring the return closer to 9%—still well short of 12%. Plus, many real-life investors don't reinvest their dividends, effectively reducing their compounding power.)

Now let's change the time period. That 5.16% figure includes the Great Depression. What would the average look like without it? From 1941 through 2001, the average return was 7.79%. Tack on 3.5% or so for dividends, and we're over 11%.

Return figures are phantoms—moving targets. That's because the figures are constantly changing—one year is terrible, the next few years are great. Or vice versa.

For example, if you could have invested in the Dow on January 1, 1994 and sold on December 31, 1999, you would have realized an incredible annual average return of 27%—more than tripling your money in five years.[6] Does that mean you should expect those kinds of returns from now on? Of course not.

"None of this bothers me," you say. "I'm in for the long haul. I can handle some ups and downs."

That's good. Because there's no telling how long it might take to recover from a massive drop in your portfolio. It could take three years, or five, or ten. Are you willing to wait that

---

[5] In case you find this figure hard to believe, my source is Thomson Financial's *InvestmentView*™ software, version 9.0. Look it up for yourself.

[6] Figure includes reinvested dividends.

long? Can you patiently watch your portfolio crawl slowly out of its hole—without kicking yourself for not selling when you had the chance? Most people would be quietly tormented with woulda, coulda, shoulda.

THE BROKER PROBLEM

Another problem with stocks is that so many people and companies have a vested interest in your transactions.

If you use a full-service broker, he probably gets paid a commission on every transaction. In general, if you don't trade, he doesn't get paid. What's more, the brokerage firm likely has a minimum production quota for all brokers to meet. Plus, there are incentives for reaching certain higher levels of production, including cash bonuses and exotic vacations. On top of all that, the firm may have specific stocks or other products that they want to push.

Is it possible that your interests might get overlooked in the shuffle?

Commissions require trading activity, even though frequent trading is seldom in the investor's best interest. Even online brokers need trades to survive. In fact, these brokers rely on constant trading even more than full-service firms do. The reason is the fact that they have lower commission rates and fewer outside sources of revenue.

They need you to trade, and trade a lot. So they pump up the volume with as many bells and whistles as possible. Real-time quotes! Analyst reports! Instant trade execution! Super-low commission rates! To stay in business, they need you to trade early and often. So what if it's not smart for you to do so? That's not the company's problem.

There is also a very nasty problem involving the stock

analysts who work for the big brokerage houses. Analysts research stocks and issue buy or sell recommendations, which the brokers then pass along to clients to create trading activity. The elephant in the room that nobody wants to talk about is this: analysts often have a vested interest in talking up the stocks they follow.

Brokerage houses are often involved in business dealings with the companies their analysts push. Publicly traded companies rely on brokerage firms to help finance public offerings of stock. Essentially, the firm buys the stock at wholesale, sells it at retail, and pockets the difference.

Here's how it works: a company wants to sell stock to the public for the first time, or perhaps wants to sell a new block of stock. As part of the stock offering deal, the financing brokerage firm receives a large block of stock to sell to its clients. The brokerage firm also happens to have a staff analyst who follows the company's stock and recommends whether the investing public should buy, sell, or hold the stock.

The firm receives the stock for a very low cost from the company, and then must sell those shares to the public. If there is public demand for the stock, the firm makes a huge profit on the sale of the stock, in addition to commissions on each sale.

How likely do you think the company's analyst is to recommend that the public *not* buy the stock? How often do you think analysts give negative recommendations in this situation? The analyst's glowing report is often not worth the paper it's written on.

As I write this, the big investment banking firms are just now starting down the road to reform—spurred on by the threat of giant lawsuits.

AND NOW THE SCANDALS!

2002 saw a host of corporate scandals. Enron, WorldCom, Adelphia and others were found to have greatly overstated their earnings for years. We learned that much of the stock market growth in the 1990's was based on fabricated numbers. We watched the news as wealthy executives were led to jail in handcuffs.

We came to believe that, not only could we not trust corporate CEOs, we couldn't even trust the accounting firms that were supposed to keep the CEOs honest. Laid-off employees lost everything in their 401(k) plans while their former bosses retired with millions. Investors saw their hard-earned portfolios wither on the vine; many swore off stocks entirely.

The long-term effect of these scandals has yet to be known, but one thing's for sure: the investing public's confidence in the stock market has suffered a serious blow.

SOME CONCLUSIONS

All this is not to say that you should avoid stocks—they're still a great way to invest. But society and habit too often push us toward stocks to the exclusion of all other asset classes. As we have seen all too clearly, investing blindly in stocks can be unhealthy.

On the other hand, if we are smart, we can make use of the characteristics of stocks to draw the following conclusions:

- Over the long term, the stock market goes up.
- Over the short term, it may go up—or down— dramatically.
- You should buy more shares when they are cheap, and sell some shares when they are expensive. (Translation: buy low, sell high.)

- There's no way to tell in advance when the ups and downs will hit.

- Since the general trend is up, you have to be invested all the time.

And there's one more thing you should know:

- There are other great asset classes with these same traits.

CHAPTER 3

Stacking Boards in Your Portfolio

Woody Allen once said, "Ninety percent of life is just showing up." This is certainly true of investing—Woody even got the percentage about right.

Actually, *over* 90% of a portfolio's return is dependent solely on the *asset class* in which it is invested. The remainder of the return comes from security selection and timing— neither of which, as we know, is very effective. Renowned economist Harry Markowitz established this fact conclusively in his Nobel Prize–winning doctoral thesis, written in 1952.[7] Markowitz' findings have been confirmed over and over by many studies in the decades following his original research.

In effect, just "showing up" in the market pretty much determines your success or failure during a given time period.

---

[7] If you want to read the full study of Dr. Markowitz' findings, get a copy of his expensive, rather intellectual classic, *Portfolio Selection: Efficient Diversification of Investments*, Oxford: Blackwell Publishers Ltd., 2000. Also in this vein is another classic work by another Nobel Prize–winning economist, William A. Sharpe: *Portfolio Theory and Capital Markets*, New York: McGraw-Hill, 2000.

A RISING TIDE LIFTS ALL BOATS

You can confirm this for yourself. Were you invested in stocks during the late 1990s, say, 1995 through 1999? If so, your stocks made money, didn't they? Of course they did, because the entire stock *market* went up during that period. It would have been hard *not* to make money on stocks during the late nineties. Ask your friends the same question—almost all will share similar stories.

Then, ask how their stocks performed during the *next* few years. Most would rather not talk about it—but you'll know the answer anyway.

Here's the kicker: when your stocks made money in the late nineties, *you didn't deserve the credit.* And when you lost in the following years, you weren't to blame. Your fate was determined by "showing up" in the asset class—simple as that.

Does this mean that it's useless to plan your investing strategy? Far from it:

- It is vitally important to *have* an investment strategy, and . . .

- You can use what is known about the financial markets to craft the *perfect plan* for you.

Most people just do it wrong. Soon, you will be able to do it right.

POSITIONS, BUT NO PLAN

Picture this: you're walking down the aisles of a large home improvement store, pushing one of those lumber carts. You're looking for materials to build your new house. As you navigate the lumber aisle, you see a beautiful 2 × 4 board—straight, no unsightly knotholes, and free of cracks. You place it on the cart and shop some more. Each time you come across a nice piece of lumber, you add it to the cart. Eventually, you have a cart stacked high with some of the finest looking boards around.

Now it's time to build your home. You've got some great boards—but no nails. You don't have sheet rock, siding, plywood, or roofing materials. You don't even have a set of blueprints. You can pile up your boards and create a semblance of shelter, but it's not going to be able to protect you when rough weather hits.

But aren't those some nice looking boards!

This analogy frequently comes to mind when I'm analyzing a new client's portfolio. The investor has pieced together a collection of stocks or funds that she has read about or been told about by a friend or broker. Each of the stocks or funds may be fine in isolation. They may have stellar track records. They may, in fact, all be excellent investments.

But how do they work *together* to form a portfolio? How will the portfolio perform in rough weather?

Chances are that many of the positions are similar to one another. There may be five mutual funds, each of which owns substantially the same stocks as the others. There may be twenty individual stocks—but they're all stocks, so they're likely to sink or swim together. There may be some bonds thrown in to the mix. But usually, little or no thought has gone in to the overall design of the portfolio.

The investor has positions—but no plan.

Why is a plan important? Let's go back to the board-stacking analogy for a minute.

If you start with a blueprint,

A good plan will prepare your portfolio for whatever the future brings.

35

buy the right materials in the right proportions, and put them together in a craftsmanlike manner, your house will keep you warm and dry regardless of the weather.

And after all, isn't that what you really want?

A good plan will prepare your portfolio for whatever the future brings. With no plan, you're taking your chances.

THE CONCEPT OF DIVERSIFICATION

Some investors actually did manage to lose money in stocks during the late nineties. The overwhelming majority of them did so by trying to beat the market. They bought into the stock picker myth and concentrated on a few high-risk, "can't-miss" stocks that eventually bit the dust.

They were not *diversified.*

Everyone is familiar with the concept of diversification: don't put all your eggs in one basket. When you invest all—or most of—your "eggs" in one particular basket, you are effectively betting everything on success in that one area. If that one area does well, *and continues to do well,* the bet pays off and you're home free.

But if that one area falters, you lose the bet. And for most people the stakes are high: their financial future. By spreading your investment dollars around, you lower the risk of catastrophe and improve your chances of success.

Most investors don't diversify well. They are taking on more risk than they think they are. They don't even realize how big a bet they're making.

Let's use a hypothetical investor—call him Bob—as our example for the next several sections. Here are some ways in which Bob might try—but fail—to effectively diversify his portfolio.

DIVERSIFYING WITH FUNDS

Maybe Bob uses mutual funds as his investment vehicle of choice (as do I). He knows diversification is a good thing, so he doesn't want to put all his money into just one fund.

So he goes online, scours the financial pages, and reads several investment magazines. He studies the funds that have performed well over the last three to five years. He checks out the funds' ratings from Morningstar and *Kiplinger's* and *Money* and *Forbes* and *Fortune* and *Consumer Reports.* Finally, he buys five great funds.

Bob's now diversified, right? Well, yes—to an extent. But probably not to the extent he thinks.

How does a mutual fund work, you ask? (If you already know, please bear with me for a moment.) It's pretty simple. You invest your $20,000 in the fund, I invest my $4,000, Bob invests his $116,000, and so forth. All the money from thousands of investors is pooled into one very large fund for the investors' mutual benefit—hence the name, *mutual fund.*

The fund has a manager who treats the fund as one giant portfolio—she may invest in stocks, bonds, or whatever the fund's prospectus allows her to. As a shareholder, you don't own the stocks and bonds directly, but you do own a proportional share of the entire portfolio, based on the amount of your investment.

By their nature, mutual funds are more or less diversified *within the asset class in which they are invested.* A stock fund typically holds from 40 to 300 individual stock positions, providing diversification within the stock market. If any one of those stocks tanks, the others might offset the loss with gains.

But that's not the end of the story.

Chances are very good that all five of Bob's funds invest primarily in stocks. Chances are also good that each fund owns *much the same stocks as all the others.* Most—if not all—probably own GE, Microsoft, WalMart, Citigroup, Pfizer, Exxon Mobil, and a few dozen other widely held stocks.

They don't have identical portfolios, and they own these stocks in varying proportions. One or two of the funds probably even holds some stocks that none of the others do. But all in all, Bob probably has five stock funds. There may not be a dime's worth of difference between them.

> **Buying several mutual funds does not necessarily diversify your portfolio.**

With his funds, Bob has essentially "shown up" in the stock market. But he hasn't really diversified, because the stock market is the *only asset class represented* in his portfolio.

If the stock market has a good year, Bob's portfolio probably will, too. If the market takes a big dive, Bob's in big trouble. So you see, *buying several mutual funds does not necessarily diversify your portfolio.*

INDUSTRIES

On the other hand, Bob may prefer to diversify by spreading his stock investments among several different industries, or sectors. He knows that industries perform differently at different times, so he learns all about them and buys a few stocks in several sectors. His portfolio might look something like this:

- *Energy:* Exxon Mobil, Chevron, Texaco, Royal Dutch Petroleum, Noble Drilling, and Schlumberger.

- *Retailing:* WalMart, Sears, The Gap, Home Depot, Walgreen, CVS, and Albertsons.

- *Technology:* Microsoft, Intel, Cisco Systems, Dell Computer, Hewlett-Packard, and Sun Microsystems.

- *Communications:* AT&T, Verizon Communications, Bell South, SBC Communications, Qualcomm, and Alltel.

- *Banking and finance:* American International Group, Citigroup, Wells Fargo, Bank of America, Hartford Financial Services, and Allstate.

- *Drugs and biotechnology:* Pfizer, Merck, Amgen, American Home Products, Bristol Myers Squibb, and Johnson & Johnson.

Bob might even throw in some other industries like food service, consumer staples, utilities, transportation, and mining. Now he's really diversified, right?

Wrong. He's still got the same problem he had with the mutual funds: everything is in the stock market.

Frankly, I'd rather have one of Bob's hypothetical mutual funds than his hypothetical stock portfolio. Sure, those are all great companies—no doubt about it. But I'd still rather have the fund.

Why? Remember what we're aiming for here: *Low-Stress* Investing. Who's going to keep up with all those stocks? Who decides what to sell—and when? And who will do the research necessary to determine what to buy with the money you get from the sale? No sir, not interested—too much time, effort and stress. Especially when there's very little likelihood that one approach will be more successful than the other.

And you know what? There's a good chance that Bob's hypothetical fund already owns most, if not all of the stocks on the list. So I say let the fund manager and her staff deal with it. You've got a life to live—don't waste your precious time worrying with the stock market!

GROWTH AND VALUE

There are two main investment philosophies when it comes to stock investing: *growth* and *value*. There generally are more growth investors than value investors, although both approaches are equally valid. Bob probably knows that growth works better than value in some periods and value works better in others, so he may diversify by including both types of stock in his portfolio.

Despite what the name implies, growth investing is not the only way to make your money grow, or necessarily the best way—it's just an *approach* to making your money grow.

The growth investor looks for companies which are growing faster or more strongly than other companies. Alternatively, the company might not be growing at all yet, but it has a new product or great idea that should lead to tremendous growth at some point in the future.

As a result of the company's present or potential growth, the stock price should grow too. The stock price may be appreciating rapidly even as the growth investor is studying the company, but that probably won't stop her from investing. To the contrary, she may well see upward momentum as another reason to jump on board for the ride.

The value investor leans more toward steady profits than growth potential. He looks for companies that are reliably profitable, that have positive cash flow, that have proven products and earnings, and that would probably do well even in tough economic times. If the stock pays a dividend, so much the better.

Since growth is often the more dominant philosophy, value stocks frequently languish at low levels while their growth counterparts are flying high. The value investor likes this scenario, because he believes that every dog has his day. While others are getting worked up over the latest high flier, he's studying the steady earnings and free cash flow of a less exciting value stock.

He'll buy his stock while attention is elsewhere, and then wait for the market to place a greater value on the company. When it does, his investment will appreciate.

Growth outdoes value in some time periods (such as 1995–1999) and value wins out in others (such as the period *following* 1999). So Bob may put some of his investment money into growth and some into value as a step toward diversification. But that's exactly what it is: a step. To be truly diversified, he still has to branch out *beyond* stocks.

What's ironic about the debate between growth and value is that, no matter the philosophy or method, outperforming the overall market is still a futile effort. That's because the marketplace is highly *efficient.*

With the wealth of information available to all, and the countless experts analyzing, re-analyzing and then acting on that information, it is virtually impossible to outdo the crowd. I quoted this next bit in the last chapter, but it bears repeating. Read it carefully and really let it sink in:

"Professionals populate the marketplace, and by definition, *the majority cannot outperform the average*"[8] (italics added).

---

[8] Gibson, Roger C. *Asset Allocation: Balancing Financial Risk*, McGraw-Hill, 2000.

> **No matter the philosophy or method, outperforming the overall market is still a futile effort.**

So, while you may like to think that you can outperform the average . . . you're probably wrong.

What about just *matching* the market—you can come close to that with an index fund. That's still pretty good, isn't it? Sure—if you don't mind the rocky ride. Low-Stress Investing is about smoothing out that ride by crafting a portfolio that's just right for you.

STOCKS AND BONDS

Maybe Bob has heard that he should include some bonds in his portfolio along with his stocks. Depending on his situation, this may be an excellent idea.

Bonds are considered safer than stocks, although they have had a historically lower overall return. And investors often turn to bonds when the stock market is floundering. That means that the bonds will probably stabilize Bob's portfolio and limit its volatility.

Plus, bonds usually pay a good dividend, which can be used as an income stream if Bob needs to withdraw money from his portfolio. And as a bonus, Bob can buy his bonds in the form of mutual funds, just as he can with stocks.

So Bob is definitely on to something here. But, of course, there's a catch.

Chances are that the bonds will limit Bob's long term return as compared to a stock-only portfolio. But Bob may not mind—the safety may be more important to him than the return. Or maybe the income is more important. Either way, he'll have to give up some growth in exchange for stability.

If only there were other asset classes that could limit Bob's volatility without necessarily holding back his returns!

There are. That's what Low-Stress Investing is all about. There's no guarantee that it will work perfectly all the time, but I think you'll agree that it's better than taking your chances with just one or two asset classes.

Before we close this chapter, let's spend just a minute on the concept that is the basis for true diversification.

NEGATIVE CORRELATION

Let's say that you had three hypothetical investments— we'll call them Fund X, Fund Y, and Fund Z. Funds X and Y tend to perform in unison—that is, when one goes up, they both go up. When X has a bad year, Y does too. This trend has gone on so long that it is well documented—it seems to happen in all economic and market environments.

Fund Z is different. Whenever X and Y go up, Z goes down. When X and Y are down, Z is up. This tendency is just as well documented as is the link between X and Y.

We could say that Funds X and Y are *positively correlated* to each other, and Fund Z is *negatively correlated* to the other two. Bob can take advantage of this fact in his investment plan. How? By including all three funds, he lowers the volatility of the overall portfolio.

Most years for Funds X and Y are good years; that is to say, those funds usually go up. But about a third of the time, they go down—sometimes way down. Fund Z behaves in just the opposite way: down two-thirds of the time and up one-third.

Bob never knows at the beginning of a year whether it will be a good X-Y year or a good Z year. By including all three funds in his portfolio, he knows that he'll never be able to achieve the full potential of Funds X and Y in any given year, because Fund Z will hold them back.

But that's okay. Because when a *bad* X-Y year rolls around, Fund Z has a good year and limits the damage. The portfolio goes up less in good years—and down less in bad years—than it would without Fund Z. Over time, Bob's returns work out about the same as if he had only Funds X and Y. But Fund Z limits the year-to-year volatility of the portfolio.

That's what we're shooting for in a truly diversified portfolio. Of course, it's not an exact science—no asset class is perfectly negatively correlated to another. But the concept does work if you go about it the right way. And you will.

REAL DIVERSIFICATION—BY ASSET CLASS

As we've clearly seen, diversification within the stock market—while necessary and good—can only accomplish so much. To be really diversified, you have to go beyond stocks and bonds to include other asset classes in your portfolio.

But what other asset classes are there? We were just getting to that. But first, let's have a heart-to-heart talk about whether you should tackle this project alone, or enlist some help . . .

Are You a Gardener or a Produce Buyer?

Investing is sort of like gardening.

Gardening isn't the most difficult thing in the world—for those who do it well. I expect almost anyone with the desire, the right tools, and enough time could eventually learn to grow his own food.

But he might starve to death while he's learning. He might not be interested in growing his own garden. He might not want to put forth the time and effort. Gardening just might be the *last* thing he would want to do with his time.

He might simply prefer to go to the produce section of the local supermarket and buy his fruits and vegetables there.

Put another way, anyone with sufficient time, resources, and desire can manage his own portfolio well. But that doesn't mean he will.

Why do you suppose that is? Probably because you really need all three—time *and* resources *and* desire—to do it well. And you need one more thing: *discipline.*

All the time, tools and desire in the world won't do the gardener a bit of good if he doesn't get outside and do the work, week in and week out. He may get off to a great start in the spring—tilling the soil, planting the seeds, fertilizing. But if he never gets around to *maintaining* his garden—watering, weeding, pruning, and fertilizing some more—his crop will wither and may die.

When autumn rolls around, his family will be hungry.

He should have gone to the grocery store.

But if the gardener *does* do everything necessary to maintain his garden, he should enjoy a bountiful harvest. He'll have the satisfaction of knowing that he did it himself. And he'll never be satisfied with the taste of store-bought produce.

For our purposes here, let's divide investors into two types: gardeners (do-it-yourselfers) and produce buyers (delegators).

DISCLAIMER

Obviously, the author has a major conflict of interest here. I make my living managing portfolios. I have a vested interest in produce shoppers.

But I also realize that not everyone makes a good client. Hard experience has taught me that do-it-yourselfers usually make bad clients—the client is never satisfied, and the advisor is miserable.

Therefore, I also have a vested interest in helping you discover your gardening self, if that's who you are. So read on, and get out a mirror.

THE MOVE TOWARD INVESTMENT "GARDENING"

Keep in mind the four things you need to manage your own portfolio: *time, tools, desire,* and *discipline.* We'll call them the Big Four.

Until the 1990s, most investors didn't have the chance to be gardeners with their own portfolios. They

> **Anyone with sufficient time, tools, desire, and discipline can manage his own portfolio well.**

simply didn't have access to one of the Big Four: tools.

The big brokerage houses had all the resources at their disposal. They had knowledge and connections that you and I did not. They had immediate access to information that regular folks had to wait days or weeks to learn—and even then, you had to know where to look and how to interpret it.

Investors were at the mercy of brokers in fancy offices because the brokers held all the cards. There was virtually no way around them. Investors never gave a thought to how much time, desire and discipline they might possess—because it didn't matter.

The Internet changed all that. Over the course of a few short years, the tools became available to virtually everyone. Now there was a way around the big brokers—you could be your own gardener.

Many people began managing their own money *simply because they could.*

But the Big Four are still there. Everyone has the tools now. But look closely and ask yourself: Do I have the time, the desire, *and* the discipline to be my own portfolio manager?

THE IDEAL GARDENER

Remember when I said earlier that the gardener would never be satisfied with the taste of store-bought produce? The same is true of the "investment gardener." If you're a gardener, you may never be happy with what an advisor can do for you —you truly think that you could do it better yourself.

But you also have to take a hard look at whether you possess the time, desire, and discipline to do the job well. If you are missing *just one* of those requirements, your garden is doomed to failure.

Some typical traits a gardener might possess:

- Prefers to do things himself.
- Wants to be in control of his financial program.
- Enjoys managing his own money.
- Distrusts others to handle his important affairs.
- Has the time to devote to his financial program—now and in the future.
- Has the discipline to establish and maintain a financial program without any assistance.
- Is able to make important decisions without consulting others.
- Understands how to craft a portfolio appropriate to his situation.
- Has realistic expectations for goals, volatility, and rates of return.
- May want to monitor his investments daily.
- Thinks nobody could care as much about his financial future as he does.

THE IDEAL PRODUCE BUYER

In contrast to the gardener, the produce buyer—while not abdicating her responsibilities—doesn't care to handle all the details herself.

Bill Bachrach is a renowned financial advisor and author from San Diego, California. In his inspiring book, *Values-*

Based Financial Planning, he talks about the differences between do-it-yourselfers and delegators:

> *One online trading company's commercial featured a classic Do-it-yourselfer sitting on a dock in front of his yacht and reciting his mantra: "Why would I pay someone else to do what I can do for myself?" Indeed, why? The Do-it-yourselfers . . . have found an ally in companies like E*trade—these discount online brokers can provide valuable information to the person who has the time and inclination to seek it out.*
>
> *But the Delegator has an answer to that question: "I pay someone else to manage my money so I can do all the things I can't pay someone else to do: exercise, go to my kids' soccer games, spend quiet time at home, take vacations, grow personally, improve my professional skills, enjoy my retirement, volunteer my time to worthy causes, meditate, read great books, have dinner with friends . . ." The Delegator's mantra? "Why would I do anything myself that I could pay someone else to do?"* [9]

The produce buyer probably has these traits:

- Is a delegator, not a do-it-yourselfer.
- Has little or no interest in managing money.
- Places money in perspective—realizes there are more important things in life.
- Has realistic expectations for goals, volatility, and rates of return.
- Wants to be involved in her financial program, but does not need to monitor investments daily.

---

[9] Bachrach, Bill. *Values-Based Financial Planning: The Art of Creating an Inspiring Financial Strategy*, San Diego: Aim High Publishing, 2000.

- Seeks a long-term relationship with her planner/advisor.

- Cares a lot about her financial future—and believes that her advisor cares, too.

- Trusts her advisor to do the right thing, but pays attention and holds him accountable.

In general, the larger the portfolio, the greater the need for an advisor. This is just common sense. A small patch of garden is much more manageable than a hundred-acre farm. If you're just starting out with a couple thousand dollars, your account will be simple and relatively unsophisticated. On the other hand, if you've just inherited a million bucks, you'll need more than rudimentary gardening skills.

> **In general, the larger the portfolio, the greater the need for an advisor.**

But don't make the mistake of considering only your present portfolio size in deciding whether to seek professional help.

WHAT AN ADVISOR CAN DO FOR YOU

I was discussing this subject over dinner recently with an executive of a large mutual fund company. This gentleman talks with advisors all over the country. He had this to say:

"The value of an advisor is tough to quantify. He should be a dispassionate quarterback, a calming influence to keep clients on the right path. I've seen many half-million dollar portfolios that used to be a million and a half. Those investors have been handling their own portfolios and now they're gun-shy, paralyzed, unable to make the decisions that are in their own best interest. They *need* an advisor. The best advisors offer a shelter from the emotions of the market."

But an advisor should do much more than just manage your money. As you read through the following partial list, keep in mind that if you *don't* use an advisor, you'll need to handle each of these tasks for yourself:

- Pinpoint your values and attitudes.
- Identify/refine your goals.
- Analyze your needs along with your expectations.
- Establish a game plan for achieving goals.
- Analyze portfolio contents and allocation.
- Prepare a personalized portfolio allocation model.
- Facilitate account set-up and transfer of assets from prior custodian.
- Monitor and service your investment program.
- Recommend and implement adjustments as needed.
- Monitor/coach progress toward goals.
- Review and modify your goals as your situation evolves.

While much of the information discussed in this book may be new to you, it should be second nature to a good advisor. If you have been investing on your own or with a high-pressure broker, you know how stressful it can be. By setting you up in a Low-Stress Investing portfolio—and calmly maintaining that portfolio—a good advisor can literally change your life for the better.

WHAT TO LOOK FOR IN AN ADVISOR

By enlisting the help of an advisor, you can take full advantage of the Low-Stress Investing concept. After all, the point of Low-Stress Investing is to allow you to live your life free of the worries associated with managing your money.

With an advisor, you *share* the responsibility and *delegate* most of the work.

But you inevitably give up a degree of control. You must trust your advisor to do the right thing, to make appropriate recommendations and follow through on his promises. If the thought of giving up some control causes you more stress, then you should consider (1) doing the job yourself, or (2) taking a hard look at why you can't trust anybody.

I've known some folks who had a hard time trusting others, and they seem invariably to be unhappy. If you trust no one, then you're pretty much on your own. That must be a lonely feeling.

Which is not to say that everyone deserves your trust. There are financial "professionals" who care much more about lining their own pockets than securing your financial future. Others, while well-meaning, are stuck in the four myths of investing discussed in Chapter 1. To maximize your chances of dealing with a good advisor, you should:

- Look for an advisor who follows the Low-Stress Investing style of portfolio management.

- Ask your friends and acquaintances for referrals to advisors whom they trust and have had a good relationship with.

- Ask about the advisor's compensation structure. There are basically two main choices:

    1. *Commission-based brokers* are paid a commission based on the products they sell to you.

    2. *Fee-only advisors* are paid a fee by their clients, either in the form of a flat dollar amount or, more commonly, a fee based on the assets under management.

USING A BROKER

Commission-based brokers are not required by regulations to fully disclose their compensation to clients, so you'll have to ask. And because you may not know how your broker is being paid, you might be under the mistaken impression that the broker's advice is free.

It's not.

Broker commissions are sometimes tacked on to your investment purchase, such as with stock trades. At other times, the commission is paid by the company that provides the product. But even then, the commission comes out of your investment in some form or other.

I personally find this model distasteful. The broker's interests aren't always aligned with the investor's, for two reasons: (1) some investment products pay higher commission percentages than others; and (2) the broker's compensation is mostly based on account activity and the sale of products.

THE FEE-ONLY ADVISOR

Another disclaimer: I am a fee-only advisor, so I naturally favor this model. I've been a commission-based broker in the past, but I believe that fee-only is the better system.

The fee-only advisor receives no commissions on investment products, but instead charges a fee that is paid directly by the client. In most cases, the fee is based on assets under management and is taken directly out of the client's investment account.

For example, let's say our old friend Bob has a portfolio with a total value of $400,000. His fee will probably be 1% of his account value per year, assessed quarterly. So four times a year, Bob's quarterly fee of $1000 (one-quarter of one percent of $400,000) is taken from his account.

Bob's advisor receives no hidden commissions or fees. Bob knows exactly what he's paying.

As the value of the account goes up and/or down, the 1% is charged on the changing account value. Most advisors discount their fees for larger portfolios.

Wow, you might say. That's a pretty steep fee. Maybe it is —if you're a good gardener. But if you prefer to buy your produce, it begins to look like a bargain.

Think of all the things an advisor can do for you. All those vital tasks can be *delegated.* What is the value of your time and peace of mind? Low-Stress Investing is supposed to free you from spending time and effort worrying about your investments.

Some people who should be produce buyers fail to hire an advisor just because they don't like the idea of paying the advisor's fee. But then they neglect their garden, and that neglect ends up costing far more than the fee ever would.

You can do this yourself. You really can. But *will* you? Do you *want* to?

So, hold up that mirror. Make an honest assessment of yourself. Decide if you are a gardener or a produce buyer. Then do yourself a favor, and follow the path that is best for you.

Now, about those other asset classes . . .

PART TWO

The Solution:
Building a House

> **You only have a finite amount of money to invest. Apportion it wisely.**

Ownership Assets

Remember the board-stacking problem we talked about in Chapter 3? The solution to that problem is (1) starting with a plan and (2) constructing a sturdy house. There are a number of materials available for you to use in building your weather tight portfolio. Let's look at them.

All investment assets can be divided into three broad categories: *equities, fixed income,* and *cash.* This chapter is about equities; in the next chapter we'll talk about the other two.

Equity means ownership. If you own a house worth $200,000 and your mortgage balance is $125,000, then you have $75,000 ownership—or equity—in your house. (Of course, strictly speaking, you own the entire house—the bank owns $125,000 of *you.* But you get the idea.)

When you buy into one of the equity asset classes, you *own* something. It may be part of a company, a plot of land with a building on it, or crude oil or soybeans. But you *own* something. That means that you participate in the full, unlimited potential of ownership. And that could be good or bad.

Theoretically, there's no limit to how high your asset may appreciate. We've all seen dramatic illustrations of this fact, such as a farmer who happens to own 50 acres next to a new highway—and sells it to a developer for $10 million.

On the other hand, ownership can carry its own dangers. The rich owner of a factory could be in big trouble if someone discovers that the factory has been contaminating nearby groundwater. He may spend years in court and be held liable for untold millions in damages. His ownership could ruin him.

> When you buy into one of the equity asset classes, you participate in the full, unlimited potential of ownership.

Fortunately for us Low-Stress Investors, our downside potential is limited: the worst that could happen is that the value of a particular asset could go to zero. That's not good, naturally—but it's a lot better than being in that factory owner's shoes.

Because there are risks in ownership, you should have your ownership dollars diversified into several asset classes. Let's look at the equity classes available to you as a Low-Stress Investor.

U.S COMMON STOCKS

Most everyone is familiar with the concept of common stock: a company is divided into millions—sometimes billions—of ownership bits, called *shares.* By owning shares, you actually own a piece of the company.

Owners of stock sell shares back and forth among one another every business day. You would expect the value of a company's stock to be determined by that company's profits, but that's not always the case. It is determined during trading hours based on the minute-by-minute trades taking place between investors. A stock's value at any given moment is whatever the next buyer is willing to pay.

As you can imagine, this process is often illogical—and it's certainly unpredictable. You can never tell on January 1 whether the market will have a boom year, a bust, or somewhere in between. That's why market timers and stock pickers have such a poor track record. But as a whole, the stock market has a solid *long-term* track record, so it's a great place for some of your investment dollars.

But here's something not everybody knows: a stock's return during a given period is often tied to the size of the company it represents.

A stock's value at any given moment is whatever the next buyer is willing to pay.

SIZE MATTERS

Stocks are frequently divided into three distinct size categories according to their *market capitalization*. A company's market capitalization (or "cap") is the theoretical *total value* of the company: if someone were to buy every outstanding share at the current market price, that person would own the entire company. The price he would have paid is determined by a simple mathematical calculation (total shares outstanding × current price per share = market cap).

A small-cap company is one whose total market cap is less than $1 billion; mid-cap is between $1 billion and $7 billion;[10] and large-cap is anything bigger than that. (Some companies are much, much larger. As of this writing, General Electric has a market cap of almost $400 billion!)

A WORD ABOUT INVESTMENT RETURNS

Reporting investment returns is a tricky business at best. It is most commonly done using various indexes of specific asset classes. One problem comes from the fact that some

---

[10] The specific range for mid-caps is open to debate. Many consider the proper range to be $1 billion to $5 billion, but why quibble over a couple billion bucks?

indexes don't go back far enough to give us a useful long-term perspective.

I have tried here to come up with the best combination of accurate indexes, all of which go back to at least January 31, 1972. Unless otherwise noted, all returns described in this chapter cover the period from January 31, 1972 to January 31, 2002; all index figures were obtained using Thomson Financial's *Investment View* database.

SMALL-CAP STOCKS

Most stock companies start out as small-caps: these are young companies just going public, with great ideas and high hopes. Of course, along with high hope comes the high risk of failure. As a result, small-cap stocks as a group tend to be very volatile—but their long-term record is very good: averaging 12.6% per year.[11]

Remember this extremely important fact: *averages can be deceiving.* What the small-cap class average number doesn't tell you is how volatile the returns have been. In the investment business, volatility is synonymous with short-term risk. Generally, the greater the long-term expected return, the greater the short-term volatility—and vice versa.

There are a number of ways to measure volatility, but one simple way that illustrates it well is to look at the best-ever and worst-ever years for each asset class. (Remember that we're concentrating here on the 30-year period from 1/31/1972 through 1/31/2002.) small-caps' best year was 1991, when they soared by almost 51%. Worst year? Down 35% in 1974. See what I mean about volatility?

---

[11] All small-cap returns in this chapter are measured by the Thomson US: Small Cap Mutual Funds index.

LARGE-CAPS AND MID-CAPS

Many small-cap companies remain small forever, but not all. If everything goes well for a small-cap company, it may grow up to be a large-cap. This category contains the great "blue chips," those companies whose names are synonymous with American business: GE, IBM, Exxon Mobil, Coca-Cola—the list goes on and on. They're in the mature stage of their corporate lives—so they tend to be much less risky than small-caps and have a correspondingly lower long-term average return. During our study period, however, their return was outstanding, averaging 12.1% Worst year: 1974, down about 26.5%. Best year: the very next year, 1975, up about 37%.[12]

Mid-caps are, as you would expect, in between the other two in just about every respect, although their returns during our study period took a back seat to large-caps. The average return for mid-caps during that time was 11.4%. Worst year: 1974, down 31%. Best year: 1991, up 42%.[13]

Why bother with all of this? Because these three categories don't always perform well at the same time. For example, in 1998, large-caps increased 27% while small-caps were losing .4%. In 2000, however, the tables were turned, with small-caps up over 4% and large-caps down 10%. There are other examples of this phenomenon, but the numbers get boring very quickly. It doesn't happen every year, but it does happen often enough to factor into your portfolio design.

Don't make the mistake of assuming that the glory days of large-caps will automatically return. They very well might, of

---

[12] All large-cap returns in this chapter are measured by the S&P 500 Composite Total Return.

[13] All mid-cap returns in this chapter are measured by the Thomson US: Mid Cap Mutual Funds index.

course. But don't bet *everything* on it—especially when there are so many other asset classes that deserve a piece of your portfolio pie.

Consider this April 2002 quote from *Newsweek* financial columnist Allan Sloan:

> *For almost 18 years—an entire generation—stocks produced returns way beyond the dreams of previous generations' avarice. From August 1982 through March 2000, the Standard & Poor's 500 Index returned an astounding 19.8 percent a year, compounded, according to Ibbotson and Associates, a research firm. This means that if you came of age during this period, you could double your money every three and a half years or so by keeping it in a boring old S&P 500 Index fund. By contrast, Ibbotson says, the S&P returned only 8.8 percent a year from January 1926 through July 1982. At that rate, it took more than eight years to double your money.*[14]

One thing we can state with confidence: investment dollars have to go somewhere. When they leave one asset class, they generally migrate to one or more others. By strategically allocating your dollars among several classes, you can limit the downside of any one class while increasing the chance of being where the growth is.

> **Investment dollars have to go somewhere. When they leave one asset class, they generally migrate to one or more others.**

We'll look at some other asset classes in a moment, right after we wrap up a few loose ends in the stock arena.

---

[14] "The New Rules of Retirement." *Newsweek*, April 1, 2002, p.58.

GROWTH, VALUE, AND SECTORS

Remember our growth/value discussion in Chapter 3, "Stacking Boards in Your Portfolio?" Both growth and value styles have their place in a Low-Stress portfolio. Some years are great for one and lousy for the other. There's no way to predict whether this will be a growth year or a value year, so you should have both.

We also talked in Chapter 3 about industries and sectors. It makes good sense to maintain a representative range of all major industries.

A WEALTH OF INDEXES

There are plenty of indexes for measuring market returns. A partial list: the Dow Jones Industrial Average, the NASDAQ Composite, the Wilshire 5000, the Russell 2000, the Domini Social 400, and various sector indexes.

Whenever practical, I like to use indexes based on mutual funds, such as the Thomson Mutual Fund indexes used in this chapter. The reason is that these indexes reflect the kinds of returns real investors have earned—and they often go farther back than other indexes, allowing us to get a longer-term view. [15]

When you and your advisor design a portfolio, you should allocate a certain percentage of your *total* to U.S. stocks. You then divide that allocation into the subcategories of large-, mid-, and small-caps. This allows you to better control your risk.

---

[15] For more complete information on the indexes used throughout this book, see Appendix 1 starting on page 135.

FOREIGN STOCKS

This category, often referred to as international stocks, is just what the name implies. The stock of any company not headquartered in the United States falls under this heading. That's a lot of stocks in a lot of countries.

Although some investors shy away from the foreign stock area because of its perceived volatility, you should probably consider putting some money here. Its average annual return has been almost 11%. Worst year: 1990, down 23%. Best year: 1986, up almost 70%![16]

Just like the U.S. market, international markets are unpredictable. Layered on top of that unpredictability is a whole set of challenges not associated with domestic stocks. Ever-shifting currency exchange rates, difficulty in obtaining accurate information on companies, and uncertain political conditions all make investing in foreign stocks a tricky proposition.

But exposure to foreign stocks adds another layer of diversification that most portfolios need. Only rarely does the U.S. stock market outperform all of the world's other markets. By participating in foreign markets in a limited way, you can potentially *lower* your portfolio's volatility while bolstering your return.

Because we are living in the reality of a world economy, the health of our market is largely linked to the markets of other countries. This means that the contrast between the behavior of U.S. and foreign stocks is probably not as great as it once was. But it's still a good way to diversify.

---

[16] All foreign stock returns in this chapter are measured by the MSCI EAFE index.

You may have noticed that large-caps, mid-caps, and small-caps all had their worst returns in 1974. Sometimes, no matter how well you diversify within the stock market, it will burn you. So the Low-Stress portfolio will diversify into other equity asset classes. Here are a couple you may not have thought about:

REAL ESTATE

This is a very underutilized asset class.

Did you know that there is a way to own real estate in an investment portfolio along with stocks and bonds?

There are actually two commonly held types of real estate securities: real estate investment trusts (REITs) and real estate operating companies (REOCs). Both are companies that own real estate in a variety of forms; REITs are more common than REOCs, so we'll concentrate on them.

REITs may own office buildings, hotels, apartment complexes, or other commercial properties. They may own undeveloped land or be directly involved with property development. One REIT could be involved in any combination of the above. The common thread is that the value of REIT shares is directly tied to the value of the real estate the REIT owns and manages.

Although REITs were out of favor with many investors through much of the 90s' stock boom, they have a long term track record worth noting. REITs as a whole averaged 9.7% in the time period we have been talking about. Best year was 1996, up about 36%. Worst year was 1974, down 42%.[17]

---

[17] All real estate returns in this chapter are measured by the National Association of Real Estate Investment Trusts index (NAREIT).

Yes, you are right: real estate's worst year was 1974, the same year that U.S. stocks performed so badly. (I was hoping you wouldn't catch that.) But that is an extremely rare occurrence. 1974 saw the U.S. economy mired in recession and Watergate.

In fact, many of real estate's up years have corresponded with stocks' down years. While the stock market lost about 12% in 2000,[18] real estate gained an impressive 26%. Those numbers were repeated almost exactly in 2001. In all, stocks have been down in ten of the years since 1972; real estate was up during six of those years.

Of course, when stocks are flying high, REITs may get less attention, and their returns often reflect that fact. But that just supports the argument for holding some real estate along with your stocks: *you never know which asset class is going to win next year.*

You never know which asset class is going to win next year.

COMMODITIES

Think pork bellies.

You can think of commodities as raw materials: crude oil, copper and other metals, soybeans, wheat, sugar, natural gas—and yes, pork bellies—are all examples of commodities. Usually, a commodity is something that has not yet been processed into a final product.

The traditional way to participate in the commodities market is to buy futures contracts on one or more individual commodities. It's a pressure cooker business. You know the guys in the wacky-looking jackets you've seen on TV, waving

---

[18] Stock market figures in this paragraph are measured by the Wilshire 5000 stock market index.

their arms and yelling frantically in the trading pits? That's what we're talking about.

This asset class scares almost everybody at first glance. And you have reason for caution: investing in individual commodities futures is fraught with dangers, not the least of which is the possibility of losing all of your investment—and sometimes more than you invested.

This is an extremely volatile area, clearly the most volatile of any class in this chapter. The asset class as a whole is measured by the Goldman Sachs Commodity Index (GSCI). During our focus time period, the GSCI's average annual return was 10.3%. But that's just part of the story: its best year, 1973, saw it soar by almost 75%—but in 1998 it was down by almost 36%.

Does something this wild have any place in your Low-Stress portfolio? Quite possibly, yes. Why? Because commodities— in moderation—may actually *lower the portfolio's volatility* and *increase its return.*

How can that be, you ask? Here's just one example: in 1974— that terrible year for stocks and real estate—commodities were up almost 40%. Wouldn't that have been a nice ray of hope in an otherwise gloomy landscape?

In his widely respected book for investment advisors, *Asset Allocation: Balancing Financial Risk,* Roger Gibson presents a convincing case for including commodities in many portfolios.[19] He shows that the GSCI often zigs when the stock market zags—so much so that the pattern offsets a large portion of the volatility accompanying other asset classes.

---

[19] Gibson, Roger C. *Asset Allocation: Balancing Financial Risk,* New York: McGraw-Hill, 2000.

Another good example of this phenomenon occurred in 2000, another miserable year for the stock market. The GSCI gained nearly 50% that year. In all, commodities were up in eight of the ten years that stocks were down.[20]

By including a small allocation of commodities—say, 5 to 10%—your portfolio might very well be healthier overall than it would be without it. By using mutual funds, you can avoid many of the dangers and pitfalls associated with investing directly in futures contracts.

No asset class is appropriate for every portfolio, and this one is no exception. But don't automatically rule it out.

CONVERTIBLE SECURITIES

Convertibles are sort of a cross between stocks and bonds. They don't fit neatly into either the equity or fixed income category, but I include them in the equity chapter because their dividend is of secondary importance to their growth potential.

If you have no idea what convertible securities are, don't let it bother you. To really understand convertibles, you have to understand corporate bonds—which we haven't talked about yet. We'll talk more about convertibles in the next chapter.

For now, you should know that convertibles are a wonderful way to largely participate in the upside potential of stocks and the safety of bonds. In the time period we've been studying, convertible securities have managed an annual average return of 10.75%.[21]

---

[20] As measured by the Wilshire 5000.

[21] All convertible securities returns in this chapter are measured by the Thomson US: Convertible Mutual Fund index.

But the beauty of convertibles is their relatively low volatility. In their best year, 1982, they were up almost 37%. But in their worst year, 1974, they declined by only 12.6%—by far the "best worst year" of the equity category.

LOOKING AT THE NUMBERS

If you enjoy reading numerical tables, take a minute or two to look over the one below. It neatly summarizes all the numbers we've talked about for each equity asset class. I've even thrown in a few more numbers you might find interesting:

- *Number of down years.* Tells how many years, out of our study period of 30 years, each asset class was down.

- *Best-worst spread.* This is the number of percentage points difference between the best-ever and worst-ever yearly returns. It's a measure of volatility.

- *Average up year.* This eliminates all the down years from the equation. In years when the class is up, this number tells you how high it goes up, on average. It's an interesting statistic, but you read it within the context of all the other numbers.

- *Average down year.* Same as above, but with the up years removed.

	Avg. Return	# of down years	Best-worst Spread	Best up year	Worst down year	Avg. up year	Avg. down year
Large-caps	12.09	7	64	37.27	-26.49	20.97	-11.11
Mid-caps	11.35	8	74	42.37	-31.17	22.08	-11.79
Small-caps	12.61	9	86	50.91	-35.13	25.43	-9.29
Foreign	10.74	8	93	69.94	-23.20	22.72	-13.55
Real estate	9.73	8	78	35.75	-42.23	21.92	-15.78
Commodities	10.29	8	111	74.96	-35.75	25.14	-19.05
Convertibles	10.75	7	50	36.56	-12.59	17.06	-6.36

SOME CONCLUSIONS

And the winners are:

- *Best average return:* Small-caps.
  Runner-up: Large- caps.

- *Worst average return:* Real estate.
  Runner-up: Commodities.

- *Least volatile:* Convertibles.
  Runner-up: Large-caps.

- *Most volatile:* Commodities.
  Runner-up: Foreign stocks.

Despite the almost-total focus by investors on U.S. large-cap stocks, they aren't the only—or even the best—place to put all of your investment dollars.

In fact, none of these asset classes has a clear leg up on the others. Every one's a winner. They share a few other traits as well:

- They have good years and bad years.

- They are not predictable.

- If you combine them in the right way, they are very likely to give you a pretty good return with relatively low volatility.

But before you get started on that portfolio, we have a few more asset classes to look at . . .

Loanership Assets

Remember the three broad categories of assets: equity, fixed income, and cash? We talked about equity in the last chapter; now we'll give a brief primer on the other two categories. Neither fixed income nor cash is as exciting as equity, but each has its place.

If equity represents ownership, fixed income and cash represent *loanership*. In these classes, you loan your money to someone else—the government, a company, a bank—and they promise to pay you back, with interest. It's really as simple as that.

The fixed income area includes all kinds of bonds, so the two terms are often used interchangeably. When you hear the term "fixed income," you may think that the interest rate is *fixed*, or unchangeable. Sometimes it is, but not always.

Bonds are a common way for governments and companies to raise money for various projects without too many strings attached. In the case of companies, they don't have to give away any ownership. In the case of governments, they don't have to force taxpayers to come up with a large amount of capital all at once.

> One advantage of bonds is their tendency to perform well when stocks do poorly.

WHAT'S SO GREAT ABOUT BONDS?

In general, most investors want one of two things from their portfolios: growth or income. Of course, growth means you want your money pile to get bigger before you start taking any dollars out. Income means you're more concerned with taking money out of the pile—without making the pile too much smaller. There are infinite degrees of the growth/income combination.

If you need income and relatively low volatility from your portfolio, the fixed income area is worth a look. Bonds' greatest attribute is their higher dividend payout relative to most equity classes. Their second greatest attribute is their safety relative to most equity classes (although this is not always the case.)

A third—often overlooked—advantage of bonds is their tendency to perform well when stocks do poorly. So you can use bonds to reduce the overall risk in your portfolio.

There are several bond categories.

CORPORATE INVESTMENT-GRADE BONDS

Here's how a corporate bond works. A company wants to raise capital for some project. Let's say Pepsico wants to build a $20 million bottling plant in Des Moines, Iowa. Pepsi certainly has $20 million in cash to plunk down on the project—but they'd rather not, so they issue $20 million in bonds.

Bonds are sold in $1,000 increments, so let's say our old friend Bob decides to buy 20 bonds—that's $20,000 which he, in effect, loans to Pepsi. (Bonds vary greatly in their terms, so let's just make some up for this example.) Pepsi uses Bob's money to help build its new facility, and in exchange the company promises to pay Bob 6.5% interest for ten years.

6.5% interest on $20,000 is $1,300 per year. Pepsi will pay Bob his interest semiannually—that works out to $650 every six months for ten years. At the end of the ten-year period, he gets his original $20,000 back.

There are a couple of wrinkles in this simple scenario. First, the bond may be *callable*—that is, Pepsi may have the right to pay off the bond early. In that case, when the bond is called, Pepsi will simply send him his $20,000 back and call it square.

The second wrinkle is that Bob may decide he wants to get his $20,000 back before the 10 years are up. If so, he can sell his bond on the *secondary market*—that is, he can sell it to another investor, usually through a broker.

If interest rates have gone down since Bob first bought the bond, he's in luck. Why? Because new bonds are being issued at lower interest rates—which means Bob's bond is paying a higher rate than investors might otherwise be able to get on a comparable new bond. So Bob may be able to sell his bond for *more* than he paid for it. (Of course, this phenomenon also works in reverse, so if new bonds are being issued at higher rates, Bob may have to sell his at a discount.)

Bonds issued by financially strong companies are called *investment-grade* bonds, because they are considered safe relative to other, more risky bonds. During the 30-year period we have been examining, investment-grade bonds' average annual total return (dividends plus market gain or loss) has been right at 8% per year. Best year: 1982—up over 43%. Worst year: 1994, down a mere 5%.[22]

---

[22] All investment-grade bond returns in this chapter are measured by the S&P AA Corporate index. Source for all index figures: Thomson Financial's *InvestmentView*™ software, version 9.0.

You may wonder how a bond can lose money. After all, they promise to return your original principal with interest. A bond's value is determined by the price the bondholder could get for the bond on the secondary market. That price may rise or fall based on changing interest rates, inflation, or the strength of the company backing the bond.

So, while holding a bond to maturity usually results in the full return of principal, bond values do fluctuate.

HIGH-YIELD BONDS

If you're struck by the similarities between bonds and bank certificates of deposit, that's understandable. Bonds function in much the same way that CDs do. But there is one very significant difference.

While the Federal Deposit Insurance Corporation (FDIC) guarantees CDs, Bob's bond is backed only by the strength of Pepsico. In the unlikely event that Pepsi were to go completely bust, they might not be able to pay off on the bond. With a strong company like Pepsico, that's a remote possibility.

But what if Bob had gotten his bond from a fictitious company called Kooky Kola Corporation? What if Kooky Kola was a young, unproven company just raising capital to build its very first bottling plant? How likely would Bob be to loan his money to *that* company?

Well, if Kooky Kola's bond is paying the same interest rate as Pepsi's, Bob will probably stick with the safety of a well-known and respected corporate leader. So what could Kooky Kola do to lure Bob's investment money from Pepsi?

You guessed it — pay higher interest! If Pepsi's bond promises 6.5% while Kooky's promises 11% — well, Bob might just reconsider. That interest rate is very enticing — Kooky Kola is compensating Bob for taking a higher risk.

That is the whole idea behind high-yield bonds. (The "high-yield" in the name refers to their higher interest rate; we also call them "non-investment grade" bonds.) These are bonds issued by smaller, younger or weaker companies. Average annual return: just under 7%. Best year: 1991, up over 33%. Worst year: the recession- and Watergate-plagued year of 1974, down almost 13%.[23]

High-yield bonds are also known as "junk bonds," but don't let the slang term "junk" scare you away. This is a legitimate asset class that deserves your attention.

BOND RATING SERVICES

Clearly, there are wide differences in the creditworthiness of companies. Some blue chip companies have billions in cash reserves, while other companies are struggling to make next week's payroll. Still others fit somewhere along the spectrum from one extreme to the other.

Bond rating services help investors know where companies fall along that spectrum. The two best known services are Moody's and Standard and Poor's (S&P). Each has its own system for rating the quality/ safety of various companies' bonds.

> The Low-Stress Investor doesn't need to learn the intricacies of bond rating systems. We should be glad someone else is doing it.

The Low-Stress Investor doesn't need to learn the intricacies of the two systems. However, it is worth noting that a bond's relative interest rate is determined by the credit rating of the underlying company. It's a great system — and we should be glad someone else is doing it.

---

[23] All high-yield bond returns in this chapter are measured by the Thomson US: Corporate-High Yield Mutual Fund index.

UNFINISHED BUSINESS: CONVERTIBLES

And now to complete the explanation of convertible securities offered in the last chapter. Convertible bonds start out as regular corporate bonds—but with two notable differences.

The first difference is that convertibles pay a lower dividend than an ordinary bond. The reason is that they carry with them a *conversion privilege* not available with an ordinary bond—and that is the second difference.

The bondholder may, at his option, convert the bond into a predetermined number of shares of common stock in the issuing company. In order for such a switch to make sense, the value of the stock usually must appreciate significantly over the market price at the time the bond was first issued.

Let's say Bob buys a convertible bond issued by XYZ Corporation. Here's the situation (hypothetical, of course):

- XYZ stock is currently trading for $15 per share

- The bond carries an interest rate of 5% for a term of ten years.

- The bond may be converted into XYZ stock at $25 per share.

As long as XYZ stock is selling for less than $25 per share, it doesn't make much sense for Bob to convert—he could buy the stock on the open market for less than the conversion price. But that's okay—because he's still getting his dividend, and XYZ will eventually give him his original investment back when the bond matures.

But if the stock price starts to go up, an interesting thing happens to the value of Bob's bond—it also starts to appreciate as other investors take an interest. (Remember that bonds can be sold on the secondary market.)

As the stock price climbs toward the conversion price, the value of the bond goes up as well. And if the stock price rises to, say $30, Bob can convert his bond into stock at the conversion price of $25, sell his stock—and make an easy $5 per share profit.

Because we covered convertibles' historical returns on pages 68 and 69, we won't repeat them here.

U.S. GOVERNMENT NOTES & BONDS

Just as companies issue bonds, so do governments. In the case of our federal government, bonds fall into one of three categories depending on the length of time the government has to repay your loan to them—and each is known by a different name.

Bills have a maturity of one year or less and are often considered a cash asset, particularly as they approach maturity. *Notes* have a maturity of two to ten years, and *bonds* have a maturity of over ten years.

Government bonds are known for their safety: they are secured by the full faith and credit of the United States government. If you put your money in a government bond, you can be very confident of receiving your full interest and principal on time.

Of course, you pay for that safety in the form of lower returns. Long-term bonds—which may tie up investors' money for 20 years or more and therefore carry higher interest rates than bills or notes—averaged about 7% per year during our three-decade study period. But they have also shown some volatility. Best year: up 39% in 1982. Worst year: down 26% in 1979.[24]

---

[24] All U.S. government bond returns in this chapter are measured by the Lehman Brothers Long Government index.

One interesting subset of this asset class is *mortgage-backed securities*. These securities are issued by federally sponsored agencies: the Government National Mortgage Association (GNMA, or "Ginnie Mae"), the Federal National Mortgage Association (FNMA, or "Fannie Mae"), or the Federal Home Loan Mortgage Corporation (FHLMC, or "Freddie Mac").

GNMA is a part of the Department of Housing and Urban Development—an arm of the U.S. government—so a GNMA guarantee carries the government's full faith and credit. Neither FNMA nor FHLMC are government agencies—they are government-*sponsored* agencies. Their guarantee doesn't carry the full faith and credit of the federal government, but the market generally considers them to be very safe investments.

FOREIGN BONDS

Many investors steer clear of foreign bonds for the same reasons they avoid foreign stocks: political uncertainties, exchange rate fluctuations, and limited information sources.

Information on foreign bonds can be hard to come by. In doing research for this book, I was unable to find an index that covered this asset class continuously over the 30-year time period starting in January 1972.[25]

But this can still be an excellent place for a portion of your Low-Stress portfolio. The United States is not the only creditworthy country in the world. There are many stable governments and many foreign blue chip companies that issue bonds. Currency exchange rates and foreign interest rates often work

---

[25] The closest index appears to be the Thomson US: Global Income Mutual Fund index, which includes some U.S. government bonds and so is not completely accurate in portraying *only* foreign bonds. Nevertheless, all foreign bond returns in this book are measured by this index.

in U.S. investors' favor. Investors can also buy foreign bonds denominated in U.S. dollars, or foreign bond mutual funds that hedge against currency risks.

The average annual return for this class has been a little over 7%. Best year: 1982, up almost 27%. Worst year: 1994, down less than 7%.

MUNICIPAL BONDS

Municipals—"munis" for short—are a special category. These are bonds issued by local governments or governmental agencies, usually for some special purpose such as constructing schools, hospitals, or bridges. What makes them special is the tax break you get on their dividends.

If Bob buys a municipal bond issued in his home state, he won't pay any local, state or federal tax on the dividends he receives from the bond. Even if he has a bond issued in another state, he still only has to pay state and local tax on the dividends—no federal tax.

So what's the catch? Low dividend rates. High-quality corporate bonds' dividends may be so much higher than munis' that Bob could pay the tax on them and still come out ahead. In order to make the tax break pay off, Bob has to be in one of the very top tax brackets—and even then it's close. Markets are funny that way—they never seem to give you a free lunch.

To determine whether Bob will come out better with a muni or with a corporate, he (or his advisor) will need to do some calculating. If Bob is in a high tax bracket, it's definitely worth the time to perform the calculations. Receiving a dividend without having to pay tax on it can give you a very nice feeling.

Because municipal bonds are really a state-by-state asset category, and because their real return is largely affected by the investor's individual tax bracket, we won't attempt to compare their long-term returns with other fixed income classes.

OTHER FIXED INCOME CATEGORIES

There are several other categories within the fixed-income area, including loan participation funds, fixed annuities, and some preferred stock. All of them have their place in specialized situations.

CASH AND EQUIVALENTS

This asset class doesn't just include cold hard cash. Savings and checking accounts, money market funds, and even CDs are all considered cash.

During the stock boom of the late 1990s, when the market was gaining over 20% per year, a slogan gained popularity among many investors: "Cash is trash." The idea was that you should have all your investable assets in stocks, none in bonds—and certainly none in cash.

Cash is *not* trash.

In fact, cash is a major asset class in and of itself. Sure, the equity asset classes are kings in the long run. That's as it should be. But over the short run — which is day-to-day, month-to-month, year-to-year—a little cash comes in very handy when your equities get hit hard.

Take 2000 and 2001 for example. Cash outperformed both stocks and bonds in each of those

> **What we are trying to accomplish is a portfolio that gives you financial security and peace of mind at the same time.**

years. In 2001—with interest rates near historic lows—cash's meager 2.36% return outperformed stocks by almost 14%.[26]

And that was by no means an isolated event. In the 30 calendar years from 1971 through 2001, cash outperformed both stocks and bonds fully nine times—almost one out of every three years. Bonds bested the other two classes five times, and stocks won the race 17 times.

But this isn't a race. What we are trying to accomplish here is a portfolio that gives you *financial security and peace of mind at the same time.* So save a little room in your Low-Stress portfolio for some cash. Long-term average return: 5.34%. Best year: 1981, when short-term interest rates were at their all-time high: up 13.07%. Worst year: 1993, up 1.71%.

LOOKING AT THE NUMBERS

As we did with the equity classes, we'll take just a moment to compare some statistics. In case you've forgotten what the numbers mean:

- *Number of down years.* Tells how many years, out of our study period of 30 years, each asset class was down.

- *Best-worst spread.* This is the number of percentage points difference between the best-ever and worst-ever yearly returns. It's a measure of volatility.

- *Average up year.* This eliminates all the down years from the equation. In years when the class is up, this number tells you how high it goes up, on average.

---

[26] The figures used to reach the conclusions in this paragraph and the next come from the following indexes: U.S. 30-day Treasury Bills (representing cash), the Wilshire 5000 Total Market index (representing stocks), and S&P AA Corporate Bond index (representing bonds).

It's an interesting statistic, but you read it within the context of all the other numbers.

■ *Average down year.* Same as above, but with the up years removed.

	Avg. Return	# of down years	Best-worst Spread	Best up year	Worst down year	Avg. up year	Avg. down year
Corp invstmt grade bonds	8.00	7	48	43.32	-5.17	11.97	-2.71
High-yield bonds	6.76	8	46	33.44	-12.92	12.35	-6.35
Government bonds	7.02	8	65	39.26	-26.01	13.19	-7.01
Foreign bonds	7.17	2	33	26.71	-6.55	8.25	-4.31
Cash	5.34	0	11	13.07	+1.71	5.34	N/A

SOME CONCLUSIONS

And the winners are:

■ *Best average return:* Corporate investment-grade bonds. Runner-up: Foreign bonds.[27]

■ *Worst average return:* Cash. Runner-up: High-yield bonds.

■ *Least volatile:* Cash, followed by foreign bonds.

■ *Most volatile:* Believe it or not, government bonds.[28] Runner-up: A virtual tie between high-yield and corporate investment-grade bonds.

---

[27] Just a reminder: the index used here for foreign bonds is not entirely foreign because it includes a minority of U.S. government bonds— but it's the best the author could come up with.

[28] To be fair, the index used here concentrates on long-term bonds, which is the most volatile sub-set of government bonds—but also has the best long-term return.

■ *Important note:* All returns reported here include dividends as well as capital gains. Therefore, if you take out the dividends each year as income, you don't get much—if anything—in the way of growth.

After looking at both the equity and fixed income classes, we can also draw a few more conclusions:

■ The worst-performing equity class (real estate) has a better long-term return than the best-performing fixed income class (investment-grade bonds)—but not by much.

■ As a group, the fixed income classes are much less volatile than the equity classes.

■ Cash is the only asset class never to have a down year.

By this time you may be asking, "How in the world am I supposed to be able to juggle all these asset classes in a *Low-Stress* portfolio?"

Good question. This next chapter contains the full answer— plus a pretty good hint in the title . . .

Investors sometimes say, "I've tried mutual funds—they don't work for me." They view mutual funds as an asset class —which they are not. Instead, think of them as convenient baskets for holding your chosen asset classes.

The Beauty of Mutual Funds

Now that you've completed your crash course in the various asset classes, it's time to figure out the best approach for getting them into your Low-Stress portfolio.

YOUR OPTIONS FOR DIVERSIFICATION

So what's the best vehicle for buying the asset classes you want? You have several options, most of which can be disposed of quickly:

- *Individual security selection.* You could pick through the thousands of stocks, bonds, REITs, convertibles, etc.—then buy and sell as necessary. No thanks— too much time, effort, and stress. (Note: This does not mean you can't have some individual stocks in your portfolio. Having a few individual positions as part of an asset class doesn't hurt a thing—as long as you stay appropriately diversified within the class. Don't lose your balance!)

- *Separate managed accounts.* You could turn your portfolio over to a money management firm that would buy and sell individual securities for you and keep you informed periodically. This is a viable option for some investors, but I prefer the mutual fund option.

- *Closed-end mutual funds.* Don't confuse *closed-end* funds with *open-end* funds, which I recommend (and which are discussed a little later on). *Closed-end funds* trade like stocks—there are a set number of shares, so you must buy yours from existing shareholders. You may have to dig around to find sufficient information on the funds you're interested in. They may trade at a premium or discount to their net asset value (NAV), so you must take this into account when you . . . Too much trouble, you say? I agree.

- *Exchange-traded funds (ETFs).* ETFs are a relatively new form of closed-end fund—they've only been around since the mid-1990's—and are just now gaining widespread acceptance. They're traded all day on the American Stock Exchange and are designed to mimic the returns of various indexes. While they appear to be a promising option, the jury is still out on their long-term viability. Stay tuned.

DISCLAIMER

Nothing in this chapter—or in the entire book—should be construed as a recommendation for any particular mutual fund. This discussion is about mutual funds in general. The fund business is highly regulated. Indeed, this regulation is intended to protect investors. All open-end mutual funds are sold by prospectus, a document that gives you loads of information about the fund. Before seriously considering any fund, you should first *read the prospectus.*

THE BEAUTY OF MUTUAL FUNDS

The mutual fund industry has given you a wonderful vehicle for investing intelligently without being consumed by your portfolio. Frankly, I can't see why anyone with less than several million dollars would invest any other way.

> **The mutual fund is a wonderful vehicle for investing intelligently without being consumed by your portfolio.**

What we're talking about now is *open-end* funds. Unlike the closed-end funds mentioned above, you buy open-end fund shares directly from the fund company. When it's time for you to sell some shares, the fund company buys them back—no questions asked.

You can always see what the value of your fund is. Share values are published daily in newspapers and online (not that a Low-Stress Investor needs to look every day).

Let's look at what makes mutual funds beautiful—along with what to watch out for.

ADVANTAGE: DIVERSIFICATION MADE SIMPLE

As this is written, there are over 12,000 open-end mutual funds to choose from. They cover every conceivable area of the financial markets. There are sector funds, growth funds, value funds, growth and income funds, balanced funds, multi-sector bond funds, emerging market funds—you name it.

Many of the funds available today aren't suitable for our purposes as Low-Stress Investors. Some are too narrowly focused; others cover more that one asset class. We're looking for funds that are broadly diversified *within the asset classes* we discussed in the last two chapters. But look at the bright side: we can throw out thousands of choices right off the bat, narrowing our focus and making our job easier.

Pick any asset class we've discussed in this book. You may rest assured that there is at least one mutual fund that specializes in that one area—and only that one area.

This is very important! Be sure to pick funds that invest in *only one asset class.* By strictly limiting your fund selections to only those funds that stay within their respective asset classes, you will be able to control the percentage you allocate to any one class.

Mutual funds are a great way to diversify within your selected asset classes. Once you know how much money you plan to invest in a particular class, you can simply buy a good fund in that class—and bingo, the class is diversified.

And diversification is what Low-Stress Investing is all about.

Caveat: Of course, nothing's quite as easy as it seems. You have to be very careful that your funds *stay* within their assigned asset classes. Funds sometimes drift gradually into another area. If one fund drifts out of its class, it could throw your whole portfolio out of balance.

In fact, many funds are mislabeled when it comes to asset class and/or style. The two leading fund analysis services, Morningstar and Lipper, frequently label funds differently from each other. One study by the trade journal *InvestmentNews* found that nearly 23% of stock funds were characterized differently by the two services.[29]

Be sure to pick funds that invest in only one asset class.

This is where a professional advisor can be invaluable. He or she can help you find—and monitor—funds that will serve their proper function in your portfolio.

---

[29] "Some Funds Defy Truth in Labeling." *InvestmentNews*, Vol. 6, No. 10, March 11, 2002, page 1.

ADVANTAGE: PROFESSIONAL MANAGEMENT

Many mutual fund mangers are brilliant investors. A fund's manager is responsible for researching, buying, and selling individual securities that are consistent with the fund's objective as stated in the prospectus. She probably has a staff of talented professionals assisting her in her efforts.

This is all these people do. They don't have to meet with clients, call prospects, or prepare financial plans. They don't have to spend all day at work and then try to scrape together the time to look at their investments. They don't have to take someone else's word as to a particular investment's value—they can decide for themselves.

Fund managers aren't driven by emotion the way most individual investors are. A good manager exercises discipline to a much greater extent than does the average investor.

In short, fund managers are professionals. Chances are very good that they will do a better job than you would.

Caveats: (1) If you pick a fund specifically because of the manager, be vigilant—just as companies occasionally change CEOs, funds occasionally change managers. Some fund companies tend to change managers more often than others. (2) You also should be wary of an inexperienced manager, or one who has very little experience in the funds' particular asset class.

ADVANTAGE: LIQUIDITY

Unlike stocks and closed-end funds, open-end funds are bought and sold in *full and fractional* shares. That means you can invest a specific dollar amount—say, $7,852.48—and the fund company will calculate exactly how many shares you should get. You may end up with 550.279 shares, but who cares?

When it's time to sell, you can cash in all or part of your fund. Let's say you want to sell $10,000 worth of your fund. The fund calculates the appropriate number of shares and sends you a check.

If you wanted to sell $10,000 of a *stock* selling at $63.47 per share, you'd have to sell 157.555 shares. But you probably wouldn't do that. Instead, you might sell 150 shares (not a round lot, but a nice even number). After paying the commission on the trade, you would end up with around $9,500.

The fund is easier.

Caveats: (1) Many funds have limits on how frequently shareholders can cash in their shares. Of course, you probably shouldn't trade mutual fund shares very often anyway. (2) Depending on where your fund is custodied, it may take up to three trading days for your purchase or sale to complete.

ADVANTAGE: COST CONTROL

A mutual fund is a business, and like all businesses, it has expenses. Unlike some other businesses, however, the fund tells the customer — in this case, the shareholder — exactly what those expenses are. The fund's prospectus clearly spells out the expenses that are charged to shareholders, so it's easy to compare funds based on cost.

What's more, with no-load funds you don't have to pay any commissions on the purchase or sale of shares.

Investors frequently wonder, how much am I paying for this portfolio? With a portfolio of funds and a fee-based advisor, you should no longer have to wonder.

Caveats: (1) Some account custodians charge *transaction fees* on some funds—it may cost you up to $35 to buy or sell a particular fund. Your choices: look for a similar fund with no fee, move your account to a custodian who doesn't charge a fee on your fund, or cough up the bucks. More on this subject in the next chapter. (2) Some funds have much higher expense ratios than others; know what you're paying. (3) Avoid funds that charge a *load*, which is a sales commission paid to a broker for selling you the fund.

ADVANTAGE: AVAILABILITY OF INFORMATION

There is a wealth of free information about open-end funds.

One of the best places to start is the fund's prospectus. It tells you the fund's investment objective, what types of securities it can buy, and whether the manager can drift out of the stated objective. It spells out expenses, loads and fees. Virtually every important fact about how the fund operates is contained in this one document.

You can dig even deeper by simply calling the fund company. Most funds have a toll-free number you can call to learn the latest portfolio statistics and performance figures.

To compare one fund to others, you can make use of a number of services, both in print and online.

Mutual fund investing is a buyer's market. One way that fund companies (also known as fund "families") compete is in their efforts to provide prospective shareholders with information. You should never worry that you can't find enough information to make a decision.

> **Make sure your decisions are based on objective, factual information that pertains to your situation.**

Caveat: In a real sense, there's almost *too* much information about mutual funds. Make sure your decisions are based on objective, factual information *that pertains to your situation.*

Advertising and the financial media can throw you off course if you let them. Don't buy a fund just because it appears at the top of some magazine's "Best Growth Funds" list. Buy it because it fits what you need for a particular asset class. Remember—you're building a house, not stacking boards.

INDEX FUNDS

One way to make sure your funds stay within their respective asset classes is to use *index funds*. Although we most often hear about index funds that track the S&P 500, there are index funds for each of the major asset classes we use in Low-Stress Investing.

This type of fund is designed to closely track a particular index. It often accomplishes its objective by buying the components of the index in the same proportions of the index itself. Index funds usually have very low expenses and are very tax efficient—meaning you probably won't pay much in capital gains taxes until you sell.

You should know that some experts worry that some index funds—particularly older funds that have held many of the same positions for decades—have large unrealized capital gains. What this means is that at some point in the future, if the fund sells some of those positions, the investor could be faced with a tremendous tax liability (if the fund is held in a taxable account). Other experts brush off this fear, saying the likelihood of such an outcome is remote.

As to which is better—index funds or actively-managed funds—it's hard to say. As we discussed in Chapter 1, it's very hard to outperform the averages—and index funds don't try. They simply try to duplicate the averages. So index funds make perfect sense in a Low-Stress portfolio.

On the other hand, enlisting a fund manager to handle a specific asset class also makes sense. He should know the class inside and out, and should be able to manage that area of the portfolio expertly. He probably won't outperform his index, but outperforming indexes isn't our goal. Our goal is to earn good, solid returns with a minimum of stress and anxiety.

SPEAKING OF TAX EFFICIENCY . . .

One of the biggest knocks on mutual funds has to do with tax efficiency. As the fund manager sells positions within the fund during the year, he may create taxable gains. Shareholders have to pay tax on those gains at the end of the year, even if they didn't sell any shares. This taxable event may occur even in years when the fund loses money—leading to more than a few grumpy shareholders.

This problem is usually overstated. First, keep in mind that tax efficiency has absolutely no effect on tax-deferred accounts such as IRAs. And second, even with taxable accounts, there's no need to stress over tax efficiency. Here's why:

To keep your portfolio in balance, you will occasionally sell some shares of funds that have appreciated while buying more shares of funds that have gone down. Unless you have a tax-deferred account, selling shares will be a taxable event—meaning you'll be responsible for paying tax on any gains from the sale.

That's not an overwhelming problem, because your investment gain far outweighs any tax you might have to pay. And if you have already paid part of the tax because of portfolio moves in earlier years, you won't have to pay so much in the year you sell.

In addition, most investors pay small capital gains taxes

out of household cash flow rather than dipping into their investment account. This allows the fund to continue to grow unfettered.

I've seen many investors sit on highly appreciated stock when they knew they should sell—simply because they didn't want to pay a big capital gains tax bill. If they had paid some tax on the gain all along, the decision to sell would have been less painful.

You pay tax on gains *only once*. So would you rather pay in bits as you go, or all at once when you sell? How much difference does it make? See what I mean? It's just not worth fretting over.[30]

WHAT TO LOOK FOR IN A GREAT FUND

Here is a partial list of some specifics. It includes several of the points we have already made:

- Make sure the fund has a record of staying strictly within its asset class. No mixed-class funds—they muddy the waters.

- The manager should be experienced within the asset class.

- If you're buying more than one fund in any asset class, look closely at the funds' portfolios. Avoid any significant overlap of holdings. If both funds hold pretty much the same things, replace one with a fund that has contrasting holdings.

- All things being equal, no-load funds are preferable to load funds.

---

[30] For a more detailed treatment of this subject, see "Penny Wise." *Kiplinger's Personal Finance*, December 2001, page 42.

> **Outperforming indexes isn't our goal.**
> **Our goal is to earn good, solid returns**
> **with a minimum of stress and anxiety.**

■ All things being equal, non-transaction fee funds are preferable to those that charge transaction fees.

■ The lower the fund's expenses, the better.

■ In general, you might want to steer clear of brand-new funds. Let them prove themselves with other investors.

■ If one fund changes the way it does business, or doesn't treat you right, there are plenty of other choices.

We've looked at the board-stacking problem. We've looked at the materials available for constructing your house.

Now, let's draw up some blueprints and get to work . . .

PART THREE

Step by Step

Here is where many investors get hung up.
Don't procrastinate.
Start now and do it.
It will be worth the effort!

Planning your Portfolio

The first step in any important project is to make the decision to do it. You're still here, so it looks like you've made yours.

But before you get too far, you need to take that decision a step further, to *commitment.* This is very important. Once you get started with a Low-Stress portfolio, you need to stick with the plan; otherwise it will do you no good.

Low-Stress Investing is a simple process—but not always an easy process. This is because it may go against your emotional grain. It goes *with* the grain of what we've known about investing for years—but for all the reasons that we've talked about, most investors don't do it.

So hang in there and know you're doing the right thing.

In the real world, most investors have at least two accounts—an individual account (or a joint account for married couples) and a tax deferred account such as an IRA. There are many other types of investment accounts as well. To keep our discussion simple, we'll assume you have only one account.

Keep in mind that a good advisor should be able to facilitate all ten steps for you—getting you closer to the Low-Stress goal.

STEP 1: KNOW YOUR COSTS

Low-Stress Investing is relatively inexpensive, but it isn't free. There are several costs involved that you should be aware of:

Custodian fees/charges. Your account must be held—or *custodied*—somewhere. The company that holds the account is called a *custodian.*

The simplest way to accomplish this may be to keep your account with a single mutual fund company and buy all your funds from within that fund family. The biggest advantage here is convenience. The problem is that you are limited to only that one company's funds. Plus, there's generally no provision for holding non-mutual fund securities in the same account. But if you have a small account, this setup works well.

I prefer to use a custodian that has a "fund supermarket." A fund supermarket is simply a one-stop source for thousands of funds from hundreds of fund families. With this type of custodian, you have a much larger universe of funds to choose from—plus, you can hold other securities like individual stocks within the same account.

Companies like Fidelity, TD Waterhouse, and Schwab all have fund supermarkets. There are others as well. To learn more about each one, call them direct or ask your advisor.

Regardless of whether you utilize a supermarket or keep your account with a single fund company, your cost to custody the account should be minimal—probably free for an individual account, $10 to $30 a year for an IRA.

Advisor fees. If you hire an advisor, you'll have to pay him or her. The usual fee is ¼ of 1% per quarter for accounts of less than $1 million, less than that for larger accounts, more than that for smaller accounts.

If you have more than one account, your advisor will aggregate all your accounts in determining the fee.

Transaction costs. Your custodian will charge transaction fees on the purchase or sale of certain securities. Most of your transactions will probably involve no-load funds and shouldn't carry transaction fees, but other transactions might.

Depending on your custodian, certain funds may have up to a $35 transaction fee associated with them. This doesn't mean those funds are any better or worse than non-fee funds, just that the custodian charges a fee to buy or sell them.

This topic bears a little explanation. As we have seen, fund supermarkets charge investors little or nothing to hold accounts. Of course, the custodian is not in business for its health—it must get revenue from somewhere. Many funds pay the custodian a fee for the privilege of being offered on its network—but not all. For those that don't, the custodian charges transaction fees.

The custodian will probably also charge fees on the purchase or sale of individual stocks or bonds. This charge is usually minimal—around $25 or less.

You shouldn't be too concerned with saving a little here or there on transaction fees—as a Low-Stress Investor, you won't do a lot of trading.

Mutual fund expenses. As we fully discussed in the last chapter, each mutual fund carries expenses. The expenses won't be detailed in your statements—they are taken out each day before the share price is published. Just be aware of them.

> **Once you get started with a Low-Stress portfolio, you need to stick with the plan.**

STEP 2: TAKE STOCK OF WHAT YOU HAVE

This is a book on investing, not financial planning. But entering into an investment program without doing a little planning is foolish.

Before you establish your investment program, take a quick look at your present situation. This shouldn't take long —you might be surprised at what you see. Most people are blissfully ignorant of their own financial situation. Depending on what you discover, you may need to adjust your present behavior in order to reach your goals.

Note: A much more thorough treatment of this subject can be found in Bill Bachrach's book *Values-Based Financial Planning.*[31] I highly recommend it. The book

> **Most people are blissfully ignorant of their own financial situation.**

gives advice on how to find a "trusted advisor," a financial professional who can help you do it right.

In the absence of such an advisor, get out a sheet of paper. At the top, write "Present Financial Situation" and the date. For each topic below, you will need the following information:

- *Now:* What does this area look like at this moment?

- *Goal:* What would you like this area to look like in the future?

- *Action:* What do you intend to do in order to move from "Now" to "Goal?"

Here are your topics:

---

[31] Bachrach, Bill. *Values-Based Financial Planning: The Art of Creating an Inspiring Financial Strategy*, San Diego: Aim High Publishing, 2000.

Cash reserves. This is how much ready cash money you have on hand at this moment. It includes money under the mattress and in the bank.

Debt. How much do you owe, and to whom? Debt will almost always be a drag on your ability to accomplish your goals, so you should do everything you can to eliminate it as soon as possible — especially short-term, high-interest debt such as credit cards.

Income. How much are you bringing in — and what is your net take-home pay?

Spending. This may take some effort — and depending on your situation, maybe a lot of effort. You should have a real handle on how much you're spending and what you're spending it on. If you don't know, examine every receipt, credit card statement and check register for the next three months so you can find out. What we're talking about here is a *budget.* If you don't have one, you need one.

Will(s). Everybody should have one — a good one, prepared by an attorney. If you have one but it hasn't been updated in a long time, go ahead and do it.

Trust(s). Depending on your situation, you may benefit from one of the many forms of trusts. Your advisor can help you with some basic information here, but you'll need an attorney to set it up. Once the trust is established, it is useless unless you fund it. Your advisor can help you in placing assets in the trust.

Retirement fund(s). This includes your retirement plan at work as well as IRAs. Get with your advisor to plan what you'll need at retirement — you'll probably be surprised at how large the figure is.

Taxable portfolio. How much do you have in non-retirement accounts?

Business value. If you own a business, you have an asset you can sell when you retire.

College fund. How much do you have set aside for your kids' education in things like 529 Plans and Education IRAs?

Home value. This is your home equity. Please don't use it to get into more debt if you can avoid it.

Other investments. Have you left anything out? Land, rental properties—anything?

Insurance coverage. Check with your agent and make sure you have adequate coverage on your life, home, cars, belongings and health. You may also need coverage for long term care. And don't forget umbrella liability coverage—it could save your skin someday.

STEP 3: SET YOUR GOALS

Now it's time to solidify your goals. Get out a fresh sheet of paper. At the top, write "Goals" and the date. For each topic below, you will need the following information:

- *Goal name:* Specify names for your goals. They could be: Retirement, College Funding, Home Down Payment, Buy Business, Travel Fund, Estate Plan, Second Home, Gifting, Semi-retirement—whatever.

- *Priority:* Where does each goal rank in relation to the others?

- *Date:* When do you intend to make this goal a reality? Bill Bachrach writes, "The future will come whether you plan for it or not. Will you have the future you want or the future that happens by default?"[32] So set some specific dates.

■ *Cost:* How much will you need on the above date to accomplish the goal? Don't forget to allow for inflation.

■ *Details:* Describe some of the goal's specifics.

You don't have to tackle all this alone—your advisor can help. But whatever you do, *do it.*

STEP 4: ESTABLISH YOUR RISK/REWARD LEVEL

This is a very important step, because it has a strong bearing on the design of your portfolio. You should not take it lightly.

But this step is also frequently mishandled. Many investors—and even some advisors—try to discover the investor's "comfort level" by completing a simple questionnaire. Each answer carries a certain score. Depending on the final score, the instrument tells the investor how much risk he can handle.

But investing isn't just about risk—it's about *accomplishing goals.* In order to achieve your goals, you will need to earn a certain return on your investments. So you should start with your return requirements.

If you need to earn a 10% annual return to accomplish your goals—but the questionnaire says you never want to see a negative year in your portfolio—you have a problem. No one can promise 10% annual returns with no volatility—the markets simply don't work that way.

The higher you go in your return expectations, the more volatility you'll have to endure. Good portfolio design can

---

[32] Bachrach, page 29.

Expectations in the 8% to 11% range are realistic and potentially attainable—although nothing is guaranteed. Be very suspicious of anyone who promises you more.

mitigate this connection to a certain extent, but you can't eliminate it.

Part of what it means to be a Low-Stress Investor is to have *realistic expectations* for your portfolio's returns. If you expect your investments to grow by 15% per year—even with volatility—you need to change your expectation. Sure, stocks grew at over 30% per year in the late 1990s—and there will probably be similar spurts sometime in the future—but you can't base your future on a short-term best-case scenario.

Even a 12% to 13% expectation may be unrealistic. Only one asset class we've talked about in this book—small-cap stocks—has a long-term average return over 12% (12.61% to be exact). And it would be foolish to put everything into a single asset class in the hope that history will repeat itself—especially a class as volatile as small-caps.

Expectations in the 8% to 11% range are realistic and potentially attainable—although nothing is guaranteed. You should be very suspicious of anyone who promises you more. Remember the old saying: If it sounds too good to be true, it probably is.

A word about portfolios whose main objective is income:

The commonly accepted rule of thumb in the financial planning profession is that you can withdraw about 3% of an account per year without jeopardizing the long-term viability of the account. This should allow room for the account to grow in most years, so that annual withdrawals, while staying at the 3% level, should be able to increase and keep up with inflation.

Even this widely accepted practice doesn't guarantee success. But if it is handled properly, you should be able to sleep peacefully at night while taking income from your portfolio.

What if you are hoping to withdraw, say, 10% from your portfolio each year? You need to understand that, with a few bad years, your plan may well stress your portfolio beyond repair.

So get together with your advisor and establish some realistic expectations for the volatility and returns of your accounts. It's a necessary reality check.

STEP 5: ANALYZE YOUR CURRENT PORTFOLIO

Warning: This is easier said than done. It's easy to get it wrong. If possible, let your advisor do it.

If you have an existing portfolio, you need to determine exactly what you have. You may have various stocks, bonds, and funds, but what asset classes do they fall under, and in what proportions?

If, like many investors, you have accounts with several different custodians, you'll want to analyze each and crunch them all together as if they were one big portfolio.

Determining the market cap of stocks is fairly straightforward. Any good financial web site can give you the current share price and number of outstanding shares. A quick multiplication with a calculator, and *voila*! (Just be sure your calculator can handle a lot of digits!)

Individual bonds are also easy to analyze. Your account statement probably lists your bonds along with the issuers, maturity dates, dividend interest rates, and ratings.

Mutual funds are where this exercise gets interesting. As

you know, many mutual funds — perhaps most — contain more than one asset class.

It may be a mistake to just lump a fund into a category based on its name. The ABC Mid-cap Fund may in fact contain a lot of large-caps and small-caps, as well as some foreign stocks. Global funds almost always include both U.S. and foreign stocks, in several market cap categories. Funds with "growth and income" in the name often contain no bonds at all, even though the name implies otherwise.

It doesn't get much easier once you start looking inside the funds. There are several services that report on fund portfolios, most notably Morningstar and Lipper. But they often disagree on the asset allocation of funds. Your advisor should have some additional resources at his disposal to complete the job fairly well.

When you're done, your advisor can put everything together into a neat spreadsheet and pie chart. Our old friend Bob's portfolio might look something like the one on the next page.

Depending on his situation, Bob's portfolio may be way out of balance. Yours may be, too.

For taxable accounts, you'll want to consider what your capital gains tax liability will be on appreciated securities. Portfolio decisions based on tax consequences are often bad decisions, but you still have to take this into account.

ASSET ALLOCATION — "BOB"

	Percentage	CURRENT Value
EQUITY:		
U.S. large-cap stocks	57%	342,533
U.S. mid-cap stocks	13%	78,523
U.S. small-cap stocks	9%	52,698
Foreign stocks	2%	10,586
Convertible securities	0%	–
Real estate	1%	3,255
Commodities	0%	–
Total Equity	81%	$ 487,595
BONDS:		
High yield bonds	0%	
Corp investment-grade bonds	1%	5,822
Other income	0%	–
U.S. government bonds	4%	22,586
Foreign bonds	0%	–
Municipal bonds	0%	–
Total Bonds	5%	$ 28,408
Cash and Equivalents	14%	$ 87,500
TOTAL	100%	$ 603,503

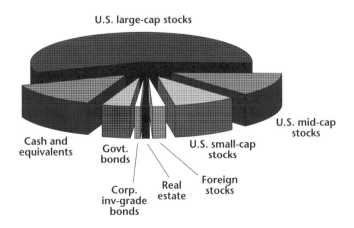

109

STEP 6: SET YOUR TARGET ALLOCATION

This is a vital step. It's where you design the "big picture" of your portfolio. There are literally hundreds of variations, most of which wouldn't be right for you.

You're drawing your blueprint here. You don't want to get this wrong.

Your target allocation should take everything we've talked about in this book and apply it to your specific situation. It should consider everything in Steps 2 through 4 above—plus your age, family situation, and future prospects. And it should take the uncertainties of the future into account.

For all these reasons, we will not attempt to design your personal portfolio allocation here. It would be a disservice to you.

Having said that, here are three sample portfolio designs —stock blueprints, if you will—ranging from very conservative to middle-of-the-road to very aggressive. Be aware that these are just three examples; there are hundreds of possibilities. Your design almost certainly should look very different from these.

Please, *don't* just take one of these and run with it. You deserve your own custom blueprint. My best advice is to get a good advisor and do it right.

ASSET ALLOCATION — CONSERVATIVE EXAMPLE
(Older, needs income)

	Percentage	TARGET Value
EQUITY:		
U.S. large-cap stocks	0%	–
U.S. mid-cap stocks	0%	–
U.S. small-cap stocks	0%	–
Foreign stocks	0%	–
Convertible securities	15%	90,525
Real estate	10%	60,351
Commodities	0%	–
Total Equity	25%	$ 150,876
BONDS:		
High yield bonds	15%	90,525
Corp investment-grade bonds	25%	150,876
U.S. government bonds	20%	120,701
Foreign bonds	5%	30,175
Municipal bonds	0%	–
Total Bonds	65%	$ 392,277
Cash and Equivalents	10%	$ 60,350
TOTAL	100%	$ 603,503

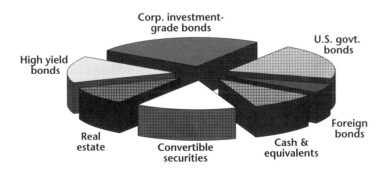

ASSET ALLOCATION — MIDDLE-OF-THE-ROAD EXAMPLE
(Middle-aged, needs steady growth)

	Percentage	TARGET Value
EQUITY:		
U.S. large-cap stocks	10%	60,350
U.S. mid-cap stocks	3%	18,105
U.S. small-cap stocks	2%	12,070
Foreign stocks	10%	60,350
Convertible securities	15%	90,525
Real estate	10%	60,350
Commodities	5%	30,175
Total Equity	55%	$ 331,925
BONDS:		
High yield bonds	10%	60,350
Corp investment-grade bonds	20%	120,701
U.S. government bonds	0%	–
Foreign bonds	5%	30,175
Municipal bonds	0%	–
Total Bonds	35%	$ 211,226
Cash and Equivalents	10%	$ 60,350
TOTAL	100%	$ 603,503

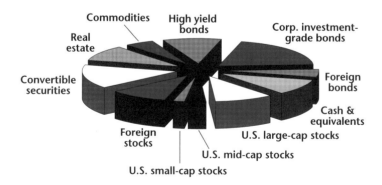

ASSET ALLOCATION — AGGRESSIVE EXAMPLE
(Younger, wants maximum growth)

	Percentage	TARGET Value
EQUITY:		
U.S. large-cap stocks	25%	150,876
U.S. mid-cap stocks	7%	42,245
U.S. small-cap stocks	8%	48,280
Foreign stocks	15%	90,525
Convertible securities	15%	90,525
Real estate	10%	60,350
Commodities	15%	90,525
Total Equity	95%	$ 573,326
BONDS:		
High yield bonds	0%	–
Corp investment-grade bonds	0%	–
Other income	0%	–
U.S. government bonds	0%	–
Foreign bonds	0%	–
Municipal bonds	0%	–
Total Bonds	0%	–
Cash and Equivalents	5%	$ 30,177
TOTAL	100%	$ 603,503

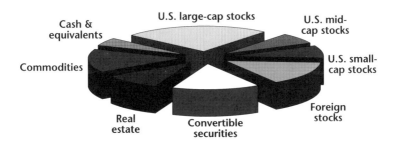

Now, let's make it happen . . .

Don't keep five separate accounts when they can be consolidated into one or two.

Keep your most trusted advisor and fire the rest.

Limit yourself to one good fund in each asset class.

Simplify—and feel the stress fall away.

Building and Maintaining Your Portfolio

You've learned about asset classes and how they can complement one another. You've done your homework and designed your big picture portfolio. Now you're going to make it a reality.

This is where you build your house. Not until Step 8 do you actually pick out your boards and other building materials. Most investors do that *first*. They end up with a pile of pretty boards; you will end up with an architecturally designed, custom-built house.

Hope you're ready for some paperwork—this is the real nitty-gritty. Reminder: your advisor should be able to handle most of this for you.

STEP 7: SET UP AND FUND YOUR ACCOUNT(S)

The first step here is to choose a single custodian for all your accounts. If you have several different accounts with different brokerage houses, consolidate them all together in one place.

Why? For starters, it makes your life simpler, and that's one of our main objectives. With everything in one place—on one statement—you can see at a glance what you have. You can easily keep track of it all. You can re-allocate your investments easily, without worrying about transferring money or writing letters of instruction.

If your accounts are with different advisors, pick just one. This should be the advisor you trust and believe in the most.

Surely there is one advisor whom you secretly consider better than the others.

With different advisors, you're bound to get conflicting recommendations. Chances are that none of them has a good handle on your overall situation.

Besides, surely there is one advisor whom you secretly consider better than the others. Why would you trust even a *part* of your financial future to someone you consider second best? Turn it all over to the best one—you deserve it.

There will be several forms to fill out. This is probably the least fun part of the entire process, but it has to be done. And it needs to be done right. As my father always said, a job worth doing is worth doing well. This one is no exception.

If you're transferring assets from another custodian, part of the paperwork will involve completing one or more transfer forms. It may take a while for the assets to transfer—custodians don't like giving up assets, so they tend to drag their feet. But they are required to follow your written instructions on the transfer forms, so just be patient.

If you're worried that you'll have to call your old broker and tell her you're leaving her, don't. Your advisor and the custodian should be able to handle the entire transfer process.

You can also deposit money into the account by simply writing a check. Whether you contribute cash to the account at the beginning or not, you should add to it periodically so you can progress toward your goals. An easy way to accomplish this is with a monthly draft from your checking account.

If you have stock or bond certificates held in a safe deposit box or at home, by all means, put them in the account. Even if you don't intend to sell them anytime soon, this will make your life easier.

Once the stock is in your account, everything becomes automated: dividends get paid directly into the account, stock splits happen automatically, and you never need to wonder how your stock is doing because your monthly statement tells you.

STEP 8: PICK YOUR SECURITIES

Decide which mutual funds you will use for each of your selected asset classes. Use the guidelines in Chapter 7, "The Beauty of Mutual Funds." Choose wisely.

If you plan to use some individual stocks for part of your large-cap, mid-cap, or small-cap allocation, that's fine. But be careful that you don't limit yourself to just a few stocks and no funds.

In order for asset allocation to work properly, you need to be *broadly* diversified within each asset class. If you own $85,000 worth of ExxonMobil that your grandmother gave you, you should not use that as your *only* large-cap holding. Yes, yes—of course it's a great company. But it's just *one board*—we're building a house here, remember?

Keep in mind, too, that small-caps and mid-caps tend to grow into the next-larger size category. Keep track of where your stocks belong.

STEP 9: ESTABLISH YOUR POSITIONS

By now you know where you are and where you want to be. How are you going to get from here to there? You'll probably need to sell some current positions, and you'll definitely need to buy at least some of the securities you selected in the last step.

To help simplify this process, your advisor may find it helpful to prepare a third spreadsheet showing the difference between your current and target allocations. On the next page is an example, using Bob's middle-of-the-road target from the previous chapter.

It's clear from the spreadsheet that Bob has to sell a lot of his stock positions — from large-cap through small-cap — before he can buy what he needs to balance his portfolio. He also needs to sell all his government bonds.

At this point you may look at the drastic nature of the change and ask: *Do I have to do this all at once?* That's an understandable question.

Looking at the current and target portfolios side by side makes you realize what a big change you're making. You're moving from a familiar portfolio to something that's quite new for you. It can be a traumatic experience. You may get right up to the edge and balk.

Let's pretend you're Bob for a moment. Remember what you're trying to accomplish, and why. You know you need balance in your portfolio. You know that being so overloaded in one asset class is unhealthy. You know your Low-Stress portfolio will give you greater peace of mind. You may even need the added income that will be generated from the new portfolio.

You can't get from one to the other without doing some selling.

CURRENT VS. TARGET
Bob — Growth with Income

	Actual	Target	Over (under)
EQUITY:			
U.S. large-cap stocks	342,533	60,350	282,183
U.S. mid-cap stocks	78,523	18,105	60,418
U.S. small-cap stocks	52,698	12,070	40,628
Non-U.S. stocks	10,586	60,350	(49,764)
Convertible securities	–	90,525	(90,525)
Real estate	3,255	60,350	(57,095)
Commodities	–	30,175	(30,175)
Total Equity	$ 487,595	$ 331,925	$ 155,670
BONDS:			
High yield bonds	–	60,350	(60,350)
Corp invstmt-grade bds	5,822	120,701	(114,879)
Other income	–	–	–
U.S. government bonds	22,586	–	22,586
Foreign bonds	–	30,175	(30,175)
Municipal bonds	–	–	–
Total Bonds	$ 28,408	$ 211,226	$ (182,818)
Cash and Equivalents	$ 87,500	$ 60,350	$ 27,150
TOTAL	$ 603,503	$ 603,503	

But then there's the possibility that many of your stock holdings are underwater—you may have lost a lot of money on those stocks. Or maybe you've *made* money on them, but they're way down from where they once were. You shouldn't sell when they're so far down, should you? Wouldn't that be breaking the "buy low—sell high" rule?

Let's look at the emotional side of this argument. We naturally want to make good decisions. When we make a good investment, we silently pat ourselves on the back for being so clever—or we brag to our friends. So what do we do when we make an investment that does poorly, or when we fail to sell an investment at its high point?

We keep it to ourselves. We don't want everybody to know we made a bad decision. Maybe it will come back—maybe one day it will go through the roof and we can feel good about ourselves again. If we sell now and it comes back later, then we've made *two* bad decisions.

So we do nothing. Selling would be a tacit admission of failure and defeat. So we wait, hope—and try not to think about it.

Now let's look at the other side of the argument. Yes, that investment might come back. But if you sell, and then use the money for a new investment—well, that new investment might do pretty well, too. Who is to say which one will do better—we don't want to get into the business of predicting the future, do we? That's what we're trying to get away from.

Try to look at the big picture. You know this: by having a balanced portfolio, you can increase your chances of having at least some of your asset classes doing well in any given time period. You won't have to worry so much, because your eggs will be spread around in more baskets.

Which is worse: admitting defeat—or continuing with an unbalanced portfolio?

So, to answer the question: No, you don't have to do it all at once. But you probably should. Consult your advisor to make sure.

STEP 10: MAINTAIN YOUR PORTFOLIO

Once you have your portfolio established, the hard part is over! Now all you have to do is keep things humming along. This is not a hard job—but it's vital. You can't just set it and forget it.

Here's what you should do to maintain a healthy portfolio:

Check your monthly statements. Just take a quick look each month to make sure everything is as it should be. If you have a question or something doesn't make sense to you, check with your advisor.

Review each quarter. Many advisors conduct in-person meetings with their clients several times a year. At the meeting, you should review the portfolio. You might want to see how the various components have fared in the last few months. You definitely want to make sure your funds are doing the job you hired them to do. Special situations, such as new management at one of your funds, might cause you to consider a change.

This meeting is also a good time to discuss other financial issues with your advisor. Are you on track to meet your goals? Are your goals changing? Thinking about changing jobs, selling your house, or buying a new car? Is your estate plan up-to-date? All these subjects—and many more—are appropriate for you to discuss with your advisor.

Rebalance every year. This is a very important step. Once each year, your advisor should redo the spreadsheets that were used to establish your portfolio. Look at both the current and target allocations. If some of the allocations have gotten more than a few percentage points off the mark, get them back on target.

This involves selling a portion of the funds that have out-grown their target allocation and buying more of the funds that have fallen behind.

Here's another point at which investors sometimes hesitate. They ask: Does this mean I have to *sell* part of my winners and *buy* more of the losers?

Look at it this way: you're not buying losers—you're buying *bargains*. From a logical, planning standpoint, it makes perfect sense. It's just the emotional pill that's hard to swallow.

This is where human nature gets in the way of good investing. We get used to seeing a particular fund go up, and we enjoy watching it appreciate. We see another fund going down, and we mentally write it off as a loser. But that winner probably won't just keep going up forever, and the loser probably won't go down forever.

Chances are that those funds are simply mirroring their respective asset classes to a very great extent. And you know that all asset classes go up in most years—but also go down in some years (except for cash, which doesn't go down).[33] You also know there's no way to tell in advance which type of year it will be.

Don't change your allocation just because a particular asset class outshines the others for several years in a row.

So by taking some of your gains off the table and reinvesting them in areas that are temporarily down, you stay in the best position to take advantage of good years in all your asset classes. At the same time, you'll limit the damage done by any class when hard times hit.

In short, *you are buying low and selling high.* And you're doing it *automatically*, because it's the only way to keep your portfolio properly balanced.

Adjust your allocation as needed. As you get older, your situation will evolve. The kids will approach college age and will

---

[33] Of course, inflation can sometimes negatively affect cash, causing a loss of purchasing power.

one day be gone. You will approach—and then enter—retirement. You will pay off your mortgage. You may inherit some money or win the lottery. Other events—often unexpected—will occur to change your life.

As this happens, it may be appropriate to adjust your target allocation. Don't do this lightly, but don't etch your original allocation in stone, either.

Whatever you do, don't change your allocation just because a particular asset class outshines the others for several years in a row. If you move more heavily into the hot class, you could be making a very big mistake. The higher it climbs, the closer it gets to a correction. You're asking for trouble if you take your eye off the ball.

CONGRATULATIONS!

You have become an official Low-Stress Investor. You have taken the necessary steps to establish and maintain your optimum portfolio. You're well on your way to worry-free investing.

To wrap things up, let's have a little talk about what it means to live the life of a Low-Stress Investor . . .

> *As in most endeavors, your success as a Low-Stress Investor boils down to one word: attitude.*

The Mind of the Low-Stress Investor

As a Low-Stress Investor, your mindset and attitude are different from those of many other investors. And it should remain that way, because Low-Stress Investing is a long-term process.

Let's consider what this should mean to some aspects of your everyday life.

IGNORING THE FINANCIAL MEDIA

No more CNBC. Go ahead and turn it off right now. I'll wait.

I know it sounds harsh, but it's for your own good. If you've been watching, quit. If you don't watch, don't start. You'll thank me later.

Let me tell you how I weaned myself from the financial media.

STANLEY'S STORY

When I was just getting started as a commission broker— before I saw the light and went to fee-only—I got to know quite a few experienced brokers, both at my firm and others. I quickly noticed a pattern of behavior shared by many of the most successful salespersons. I developed in my mind's eye a role model, the ideal broker. I called him Stanley.

Although this character was fictitious, his traits and methods were based on dozens of real-life Stanleys. Every local brokerage office had one during the go-go market of the 1990s. Stanley was, as they say in the sales business, a machine. He would get up early each morning and eat a healthy breakfast while reading the financial papers and checking out overnight events on CNBC, television's pre-eminent network for business news. After a quick workout, he'd be off to the office.

At about 10:00 a.m. Stanley would stroll into his office with the *Wall Street Journal* under his arm. He would greet everyone with a pleasant smile, tune his desktop television to CNBC, and start dialing for dollars. He would make call after call to clients, friends, even strangers. When he got someone on the phone, he would exchange brief pleasantries and then get right to the pitch. He was an incredible salesman.

He always had one obscure stock of the moment—which he had researched thoroughly. His charming personality, his persistent salesmanship, and his utter belief in his chosen stock combined to produce five to ten sales each day. Stanley cleared a cool $100 to $200 on each transaction. By 3:00 p.m., he'd be heading out the door with a smile and a wave. He spent the rest of the day and most of the evening reading financial magazines and watching—you guessed it—CNBC.

Stanley's little TV buzzed all day with the constant drone of reporters, analysts, anchors and guests as they picked apart every detail of the day's events. In his sales pitch to clients, Stanley would often use some tidbit he had heard earlier in the day. The underlying message was clear: Stanley had his finger on the pulse of the market, and they'd better buy while the buying was good.

A few months later, he'd call everyone back and urge them to sell so they could buy his next hot tip.

Stanley was the office expert. He knew what economists were saying, what direction interest rates were likely to head, what the consensus earnings estimate was on any given stock, even which companies were the subject of takeover rumors. During sales meetings, the head broker would ask Stanley some probing question such as, "Stanley, how do you think the Fed meeting will affect the market today?" He'd respond in an equally pithy way, such as, "Oh, I think twenty-five basis points are already priced into the market."

For a while I thought this was *the* way to invest. So I got a small television for my desk and, like a good Stanley, tuned it to CNBC. I read the financial papers and websites. When someone asked me a question about interest rates or earnings estimates or market PE ratios, I'd be ready with an answer, often something pithy like, "Oh, I think that's already priced into the market." I learned a lot.

But I still didn't know as much as a Stanley should, so instead of a hot stock, I sold a stock mutual fund to everyone who would listen to me. It took a lot less effort and expertise on my part.

And do you know what? My fund performed *better* than Stanley's stocks. Not because of my expertise — or the fund manager's. It was because the *market* was going up at that time, and even though the majority of Stanley's stocks did well, some went down. The diversified fund carried the day.

I eventually came to realize an unavoidable truth: the constant tracking of every nuance of the market did absolutely no good. It was just so much white noise, a backdrop against which Stanleys everywhere looked better performing their sales act.

And I realized something else. A lot of my role models never stopped to learn about their customers. Very seldom did I hear a Stanley ask about clients' personal values, financial state, income needs, tax bracket, or any of a hundred things that could determine whether the hot stock would be an appropriate addition to their portfolio. Stanleys were just trying to make a sale. And by that measure they were very successful, earning hundreds of thousands of dollars a year as well as sales awards, trips, and the admiration of guys like me.

Not only did these people have their clients hoodwinked, they had performed the ultimate trick—they had hoodwinked themselves. I didn't want that to happen to me.

I turned off CNBC, replaced it with CNN, and stopped listening to market gurus. I set out on the quest that eventually led to the information set forth in this book.

Today I still keep up with what's going on in the business world. But my sources are different—and my focus is different. Which funds represent their asset classes most effectively? Which allocation models work best for various clients? How can I better help clients reach their goals? How might national and world events impact the planning I do with clients? By filtering out useless and distracting information, I am able to focus on that which is important.

Both my clients and I have been the better for it. Their portfolios are much healthier than they were before. When someone asks, "What did the market do today?"—I simply answer, "I don't know." I really don't—and it doesn't matter.

I still have a few clients who try to time the market against my counsel. I've never seen one succeed. Invariably, they are frustrated and dissatisfied. Frankly, I don't know why they stay with me.

It's not worth it, my friend. A Low-Stress Investor doesn't watch the market every hour. Or every day or week. She doesn't try to keep up with the latest developments in the investment world. It's time-consuming and counterproductive. It distracts your attention from more important things, like maintaining a healthy portfolio. You know you can't predict the markets, and you know that short-term trends don't affect the way you handle your portfolio. What possible good can come from keeping up with the latest tick?

YOUR WORRY-FREE PORTFOLIO

If you have followed the ten steps set forth in the last two chapters, you can relax. You can pretty much ignore your portfolio except to look at it periodically, and rebalance once a year. Of course, as your situation changes over time, you will occasionally need to adjust your allocation to reflect those changes.

Most investors neglect their portfolios and feel guilty about it. They have reason to worry—there's a good chance that their portfolio isn't appropriate for them. But as a Low-Stress Investor, yours is. So you're not neglecting your portfolio, you're just letting it do its thing. You should feel good about that.

You don't spend a lot of time on your investment program, but you don't have to. You spend *enough* time to maintain it properly. By doing so, you're keeping your life in balance. You should feel good about that, too.

You should never wonder whether your portfolio is right for you. Know that it is. You should also feel confident that each element of your portfolio is in the capable hands of a professional mutual fund manager.

Don't try to pick stock "winners"—you know that's not possible, at least not consistently. There's really no need to hold individual stocks in your portfolio at all—they reduce the degree of diversification and require you to decide when to sell them. And if you don't expect to *ever* sell them, then what good are they to you?

With the Low-Stress Investing method, you don't have to worry about buying and selling decisions—they're built in to the system. By selling a bit when the asset has appreciated and buying a bit when it has depreciated, you automatically take advantage of market swings. And you never overreact.

I would hope that by now you aren't trying to beat the market averages, or that you won't somehow feel inferior if the stock market has a great year while your portfolio just putters along. Remember, slow and steady wins the race. *Better a steady dime than a rare dollar.* If the market tanks, you should be in much better shape than the average investor.

You are free of unrealistic growth expectations. You aren't trying to get rich quick. If your portfolio has a lackluster year when stocks are booming, the worst thing you could possibly do is to scrap your program and jump on the bandwagon.

Your investment program is simple—but not too simple. It is the result of time-tested, proven research. It will work for you. You just have to let it.

What about the possibility of some terrible world event such as September 11, 2001? Don't worry that unforeseen disasters may decimate your portfolio. There's nothing you can do to prevent them. Just be secure in the knowledge that your portfolio is designed in such a way that you are as prepared as you can possibly be.

Keep track of returns, but don't be driven by them.

YOU AND YOUR ADVISOR

If you are truly going to be a Low-Stress Investor, you should have an advisor whom you trust to help you make important decisions and keep you on track to meet your goals. You should never feel like you have to go it alone.

Together with your advisor, you will map out a plan to reach financial security. You should check your progress periodically, so you don't have to wonder how you're doing.

With a good advisor, you have a hand in managing your portfolio, but you're not on your own. Your advisor is there as a partner to share some of the burden. Let him handle the mundane tasks that you could handle for yourself but don't want to.

You should never have to question the motivation of your advisor. If you think he's more concerned with his

> **You can pretty much ignore your portfolio except to look at it periodically, and rebalance once a year.**

interests than yours, get rid of him. You shouldn't wonder what you're paying for your investment program. With a good advisor, you know precisely how much you're paying, and to whom.

The fact that you have an advisor doesn't mean that you abdicate your authority or responsibility. Remember, this should be an equal partnership. But you're not dependent on any one individual for your financial security. The advisor advises; *you* decide.

AVOIDING DISTRACTIONS

There are tons of potential distractions out there. Part of the beauty of Low-Stress Investing is that you can brush them aside as minor annoyances. A Low-Stress Investor sees the

> **Your investments have importance only to the extent that they advance the major priorities of your life.**

world clearly. Information overload has no effect on you—you don't even pay attention to it.

Ignore the white noise of the financial press. Financial news has relevance only to the extent that it affects your daily life and the lives of those you care about. A Low-Stress Investor couldn't care less about real-time quotes, analyst reports, or earnings estimates.

Develop a keen mental filter to deal with information overload. Most of what you hear and read in the financial media can be ignored. Learn to separate the wheat from the chaff. You can start with not worrying about what the stock market is doing every minute of the trading day. In a well-balanced portfolio, stocks represent a minority of the assets represented. The swing of a few Dow points—or a few hundred—will not make or break you.

Be aware that Low-Stress Investing is not the norm for most investors. Others may think you're strange because they have fallen victim to the media. You are liberated from that mindset. The fact that others are bound by conventional wisdom does not bother you at all.

If your friends tell you to jump off a cliff, you can simply say, "No thanks."

LIFE IN GENERAL

This book has been about more than just investing. In the Introduction, "Keeping Money in Perspective," we talked about balance. Everything has its proper place in the big picture that is your life. Your portfolio is no exception.

Your investments have importance only to the extent that

they advance the major priorities of your life. Spend time on those important priorities without worrying that you're neglecting your financial health—because you aren't.

So we end where we began. Keep your priorities straight. Give your portfolio as much importance as it needs and deserves—but no more.

SOME FINAL ENCOURAGEMENT

Know that your investment plan is right for you. Maintain that quiet sense of self-satisfaction. Stay the course.

Be secure in the knowledge that you've tackled this particular part of your life. You have it under control. You have a system for keeping it under control.

Now feel free to focus on more important things.

Two roads diverged in a wood, and I —
I took the one less traveled by,
And that has made all the difference.

from "The Road Not Taken"
by Robert Frost

APPENDIX 1

About the Market Indexes Used in this Book

Market indexes can be deceiving. Widely used indexes show the sterile numbers of their respective asset classes—but real investors don't invest in sterile numbers. Investors' results are affected by indecision, inconsistent behaviors, mutual fund expenses, trading costs, and countless other influences. In short, indexes often have little relation to the experience of real investors.

In selecting the indexes used for various asset classes, I have attempted to reflect as closely as possible the experience of real investors. So wherever possible, I have used Thomson's mutual fund indexes. While they may not be pure reflections of their respective asset classes, they do reflect the experiences of real investors.

Thomson Financial is a company that provides products and services to financial professionals and institutions. One of their products is *InvestmentView*, a software database consisting of data on 545 indexes and over 12,000 open-end mutual funds.

I have subscribed to *InvestmentView* for a number of years and have always been favorably impressed by the quality and objectivity of the data it provides. It includes in-depth information on all the familiar indexes as well as 270 proprietary

Thomson indexes. Among these are the mutual fund asset class indexes used in *Low-Stress Investing*.

Mutual fund expenses and asset class impurity are part and parcel of these Thomson indexes. From my point of view, that's what makes them so useful—because that's how real people invest.

When comparing historical indexes, the period studied should go back as many years as possible so as to provide the most complete historical picture. But to make the comparison fair, the study periods for each index must all start and end on the same dates.

As an example, the Dow Jones Industrial Average dates back to the early twentieth century—but that fact is useless in comparing the Dow to the Goldman Sachs Commodity Index, which didn't start until 1970. My study period was therefore limited by the index with the shortest history.

In this case that index with the shortest history was NAREIT, whose beginning date according to Thomson was January 31, 1972. The Goldman Sachs Commodity, MSCI EAFE, and Thomson Global Income Mutual Fund indexes all started within three years prior to NAREIT. None of those four asset classes have an alternative index that dates prior to 1972.

If there had been Thomson indexes dating back at least 30 years for all of the asset classes discussed in this book, I would have used them. Unfortunately, in several classes, there were not. Most of those asset classes had only one index that covered at least 30 years, so my choice was made for me.

Following is a list of the asset classes I use in the text. The quoted passage following each index is Thomson's description from *InvestmentView*.

Wilshire 5000 Total Market Index. "The Wilshire 5000 Index Total Return is an index of over 5,000 listed and unlisted stocks weighted by capitalization, including reinvested dividends, traded on the New York Stock Exchange, American Stock Exchange and Over the Counter. The stocks represented in this index may experience loss of invested principal and are subject to investment risk."

S&P 500 Composite. "S&P 500 Composite is an unmanaged market capitalization weighted price index composed of 500 widely held common stocks listed on the New York Stock Exchange, American Stock Exchange and Over the Counter. The stocks represented in this index involve investment risks which may include the loss of principal invested."

Dow Jones Industrial Average. "Dow Jones Industrial Principal is an unmanaged price weighed index of 30 of the largest, most widely held stocks traded on the NYSE. The index represents principal only and does not include the effect of reinvestments. The index is the sum of the current market price of the 30 stocks divided by a number that has been adjusted to take into account stock splits and changes in stock composition. This index represents asset types which are subject to risk, including loss of principal."

Thomson US: Small Cap Mutual Funds. "Thompson US: Small Cap–MF is an equal weighted index of mutual funds within the stated investment category. Funds in this category seek maximum capital appreciation, by investing primarily in stocks of domestic small companies, as determined by market capitalization. Typically, capitalizations under $1 billion are classified as small capitalization companies. The funds represented in this index involve investment risks which may include the loss of principal invested. This index represents the component funds at closing net asset value and includes all annual asset-based fees and expenses charged on those funds, including management and 12b-1 fees."

Thomson US: Mid Cap Mutual Funds. "Thomson US: Mid Cap—MF is an equal weighted index of mutual funds within the stated investment category. Funds in this category seek maximum capital appreciation, by investing primarily in stocks of domestic medium size companies, as determined by market capitalization. Typically, capitalizations between $1 billion and $5 billion are ranked as medium capitalization companies. The funds represented in this index involve investment risks which may include the loss of principal invested. This index represents the component funds at closing net asset value and includes all annual asset-based fees and expenses charged on those funds, including management and 12b-1 fees."

MSCI EAFE Equity Index. "MSCI EAFE is an international index that includes stocks traded on 16 exchanges in Europe, Australia and the Far East, weighted by capitalization. This index represents asset types which are subject to risk, including loss of principal. International stocks are subject to additional risks which include currency risk and varying accounting standards."

NAREIT. "The National Association of Real Estate Investment Trusts (NAREIT), All REIT—Total Return (price and income) index to include all 211 REITs currently trading on the New York Stock Exchange, the NASDAQ National Market System and the American Stock Exchange. Due to market fluctuation, real estate investments and mortgages may experience loss of invested principal, are subject to investment risk and are considered illiquid."

Goldman Sachs Commodity Index. "Goldman Sachs Commodity Index is a world-production weighted total return index, including reinvested dividends, measuring investor returns from a fully-collateralized commodity futures investment. Due to market fluctuation, the commodities represented by this index may experience loss of invested principal and are subject to investment risk."

Thomson US: Convertible Mutual Funds. "Thomson US: Convertible–MF is an equal weighted index of mutual funds within the stated investment category. Funds in this category invest at least 65% in convertible securities. Convertible securities are bonds or preferred stocks that are exchangeable for a set number of shares of common stock. The funds represented in this index involve investment risks which may include the loss of principal invested. This index represents the component funds at closing net asset value and includes all annual asset-based fees and expenses charged on those funds, including management and 12b-1 fees."

S&P AA Corporates. "S&P AA Corporate is a Standard and Poor's long-term corporate bond index. The bonds represented by this index involve investment risks, including default and loss of principal."

Thomson US: Corporate-High Yield Mutual Funds. "Thomson US: Corp–High Yield–MF is an equal weighted index of mutual funds within the stated investment category. Funds in this category seek high current income by investing a minimum of 65% of its assets in generally low-quality corporate debt issues. The funds represented in this index involve investment risks which may include the loss of principal invested. This index represents the component funds at closing net asset value and includes all annual asset-based fees and expenses charged on those funds, including management and 12b-1 fees."

Lehman Brothers Long Government. "Lehman Brothers Govt is an index of all publicly-issued long-term government debt securities. Average maturity of 23–25 years. This index represents asset types which are subject to risk, including loss of principal."

Thomson US: Global Income Mutual Funds. "Thomson US: Global Income–MF is an equal weighted index of mutual funds within the stated investment category. Funds in this category seek high current income by investing a minimum of 65% of its assets fixed-income securities issued by domestic and/or foreign governments. The funds represented in this index involve investment risks which may include the loss of principal invested. This index represents the component funds at closing net asset value and includes all annual asset-based fees and expenses charged on those funds, including management and 12b-1 fees."

U.S. 30-day Treasury Bills. "U.S. 30-day Treasury Bills is an index based upon the average monthly yield of 30-Day Treasury Bills. Treasury Bills are secured by the full faith and credit of the U.S. government and offer a fixed rate of return."

Recommended Reading

Smart Couples Finish Rich: 9 Steps to Creating a Rich Future for You and Your Partner
by David Bach

Smart Women Finish Rich: 9 Steps to Achieving Financial Security and Funding Your Dreams
by David Bach

Values-Based Financial Planning: The Art of Creating an Inspiring Financial Strategy
by Bill Bachrach

Common Sense on Mutual Funds: New Imperatives for the Intelligent Investor
by John C. Bogle

How Mutual Funds Work
by Albert J. Fredman, Russ Wiles, and A. Michael Lipper

Simple Asset Allocation Strategies: Easy Steps for Winning Portfolios
by Roger C. Gibson

Asset Allocation: Balancing Financial Risk
   by Roger C. Gibson

*A Purely American Invention: The U.S. Open-End Mutual
   Fund Industry*
   by Lee L. Gremillion

Cashflow Quadrant: Rich Dad's Guide to Financial Freedom
   by Robert T. Kiyosaki

*Rich Dad, Poor Dad: What the Rich Teach Their Kids About
   Money — That the Poor and Middle Class Do Not!*
   by Robert T. Kiyosaki

*Crashproof Your Life: A Comprehensive, Three-Part Plan for
   Protecting Yourself from Financial Disasters*
   by Thomas A. Schweich, Kate Kelly

*The Millionaire Next Door: The Surprising Secrets of America's
   Wealthy*
   by Thomas J. Stanley, Ph.D. and William D. Danko, Ph.D.

Index

About the Author

 Andy Millard has made a career out of breaking new ground. After graduating with honors from Presbyterian College and earning a Master's degree at Wake Forest University, he quickly became North Carolina's first full time junior high school drama teacher.

Viewing his subject less as art than a means to teach discipline and self-confidence, Andy entered his young students in regional play contests—in the *senior* high division. He and his students earned surprising success, winning dozens of awards at the regional and state levels against more experienced competition.

After spending several years as an assistant principal, Andy was recruited—at the age of 35—to be the first principal of a brand-new consolidated high school. His challenges involved not only combining two widely diverse faculties and student bodies but also designing a totally new grading system to go along with a leading-edge curriculum.

Upon leaving education for financial services, Andy again chose the road less traveled, turning down offers from major brokerage firms in order to serve clients according to his own vision as an independent advisor. He has spent years researching the information set forth in *Low-Stress Investing*.

Andy Millard is a principal owner of Main Street Financial Group, an insurance agency and registered investment advisory firm. He lives in Columbus, North Carolina with his wife and son.

For a more detailed and personal view of the author, see the section titled "My Story" in the Introduction.

Do you have questions or comments for the author?
You may reach him in several ways:

Email: camillard@alltel.net

Phone: 828-859-2288

Post: Andy Millard
Main Street Financial Group, Inc.
22 North Trade Street
Tryon, NC 28782

Order Form

Fax: 828-859-6144. Use this form.

Telephone: Call 800-859-6270 toll-free. Have your credit
card ready.

E-mail: camillard@alltel.net
Include the information requested below.

Postal orders: Trade Street Publishing, LLC
Attn: Orders, P.O. Box 774
Tryon, NC 28782

Please send me additional copies of *Low-Stress Investing:*

Qty: _____ × $14.95 each = _____ subtotal

Sales tax: Please add 6.5% for orders shipped to North Carolina
addresses.

Shipping: Within U.S.: Add $3.00 for first book and $2.00 for
each additional. For five or more books add only $10.00 for
shipping. Allow 2–3 weeks for shipping.
International: $9.00 for first book and $5.00 each additional.

For orders of more than 20 books please call us for a quote.

TOTAL PAYMENT: $ _____

❑ I am interested in the author's portfolio advisory service.

Name _____

Address _____

City _____ State _____ Zip _____

E-mail _____

Phone _____

Payment: ❑ Check (payable to Trade Street Publishing)
❑ Visa   ❑ MasterCard

Card number _____

Name on card _____ Exp. _____